SELLING
without
sleaze

A Business Owner's Guide to Sales
(For Those Who Would Rather Not...)

SELLING

without

sleaze

A Business Owner's Guide to Sales
(For Those Who Would Rather Not...)

SARAH JOLLEY-JARVIS

Published by Best Seller Publishing®, Pasadena, CA
Best Seller Publishing® is a registered trademark.
Printed in the United States of America.
ISBN: **9798518107694**

For more information, please write:
Best Seller Publishing®
253 N. San Gabriel Blvd, Unit B
Pasadena, CA 91107
or call 1 (626) 765-9750
Visit us online at: www.BestSellerPublishing.org

THIS IS DEDICATED TO
MY AMAZING HUSBAND MARTIN
FOR HIS UNWAVERING SUPPORT AND
BRINGING OUT THE BEST IN ME
AND CLARA, ETHAN AND ISAAC
FOR MOTIVATING ME AND BEING MY 'WHY'.

TABLE OF CONTENTS

ENDORSEMENTS

MIKE BUONTEMPO, CEO & FOUNDER, CLIENT ACCELERATORS:

I highly recommend you check out this book where Sarah talks through her non-sleazy sales technique. I've worked with Sarah and her husband over the past 18 months; the leaps and bounds that they've made in their agency has been incredible, and one of the main reasons is because of how good they are at sales, how ethical they are. They really know what they're doing. Sarah really knows how to sell in a way where she's not pushy, gets her point across, and actually gets them signing on the dotted line.

HAYLEY FIELD, FOUNDING DIRECTOR, FOOD NINJA:

With Sarah's guidance and support, and using many of the principles she outlines in this book, my business has grown more in the past 18 months than my previous five years in business.

LISA MONGER, FOUNDER & MANAGING DIRECTOR, REBEL HEALTH:

If you want to improve your sales without all of its sleazy connotations, starting off with this book is an awesome step. Working with Sarah has been a brilliant experience and using the techniques in this book saw me increase my sales by 200 percent. A must-read for business owners.

DAWN SACH, BUSINESS DEVELOPMENT MANAGER, CONVATEC:

I have known Sarah for 15 years both in a professional capacity, as colleagues in various senior sales roles in the medical industry, and as a friend. She has always put the customer at the centre of what she does and has always been ethical.

Sarah is a highly motivated and determined person, who always does everything to the highest standards.

Sarah is a caring and intelligent individual who looks for the positives in every situation and will go the extra mile to ensure those around her are supported and motivated to be their best.

Sarah is a very astute business person, with an eye for finding the true potential in her projects. She expects high standards and enthusiasm from those around her and in return will give the same. Sarah is a great person to know, is exciting and adventurous and not afraid to take a risk in life, whilst always being there 100 percent for her friends and family.

SHONDELLE RHODEN, FOUNDER, GRASSHOPPERS:

Sarah provides so much more than just traditional business mentoring. She has an amazing way of connecting with people, a genuine person with a genuine passion for your goals and aspirations.

Her knowledge, focus, and solid methodology is invaluable for seeing the business results you dream of but without all the overwhelm.

She is part strategist, part thought provoker, and part cheerleader.

I can't thank her enough for the difference she's made to me and my family's dreams.

CAROL MURDOCH, DIRECTOR & TUTOR, CAROL'S TUTORING:

Sarah has a unique way of quickly and easily understanding your business and helping you realise how to move to the next level, and the knowledge and experience to be able to guide you in this. Her support ensured my business has continued to grow and develop, resulting in us helping over a quarter of a million children last year. That simply would not have been possible without Sarah.

SHIRA SZABO DPHIL (OXON), CO-FOUNDING DIRECTOR, FOREGROUNDS:

Sarah gave me the tools and the confidence, following some of the principles outlined in this book, to move out of academia and into practice. Enabling me to define myself in the industry of real estate and development, solidify my professional identity, present my unique capabilities and services to potential clients and to seek out opportunities to develop a new business. If you want to grow your own business this book truly is a great place to start.

JESSICA LORIMER, B2B SALES EXPERT, JESSICA LORIMER:

It's rare that I come across another sales coach that I like and trust to deliver sensible sales content in an engaging way that works for their audience. But Sarah is that person. She's smart and teaches a solid approach to sales that works well for her clients — I'm proud to be part of her peer group and know that her book will impact thousands of entrepreneurs positively.

JADE PARKINSON-HILL, FOUNDER, THE LIVE STREAMING CLASSROOM, STEAM SCHOOL:

I hadn't completed any sales training or mentoring before working with Sarah. Previously I relied on my charm and a very chaotic approach to selling. I look back at my sales approach before I met Sarah, and I honestly don't know how my business did so well.

During the summer of 2019 I grew my business organically to create enough revenue to fund the development of an EdTech platform. Working with my tech partners and launching the platform took every ounce of my creative energy, and I made the classic bootstrapper mistake of neglecting my pipeline whilst in the development/launch phases.

To be transparent, by the winter of 2019/2020, I was burned out, lost, and ready to give up on it all.

As a creative person, I need a system for everything. Otherwise, I get distracted too easily. Sarah taught me a super sales system and how to create a healthy pipeline. She also helped me to create a second income stream.

Working with Sarah has been transformative for me and my business.

I can't recommend Sarah highly enough.

PHYLLIS MARTIN, FOUNDER & CO-DIRECTOR, TRUFFLEPIG:

Selling the Sarah Jolley-Jarvis way is satisfying. My business has grown from following her approach, but also my confidence. It's so good to make something that was so challenging fun – and profitable.

VENARD FONG, FOUNDER, PAIN NINJA:

When I want an unfair advantage over my competition and to make sales without any hint of scumminess and manipulation, I turn to Sarah. In the short time I worked with Sarah, I had my two best ever months, consecutively. The lower month was a 60 percent increase from my previous best...from a year ago.

FOREWORD

DAN MEREDITH, BESTSELLING AUTHOR OF
HOW TO BE F*CKING AWESOME

I'm going to start this foreword with something a little different, but I promise it will make sense when you get to the end.

You are not special.

Neither is Sarah.

And neither am I, for that matter.

Motivational, eh? Let me explain.

As of this writing, I've known Sarah for over two years and had the pleasure of mentoring her for that period of time. She is a normal person, married, three kids, two dogs, and all the life responsibilities that come with that. Yet, I have seen her not only sell life-changing content to her clients but also grow her own business.

She has worked with hundreds of individuals who 'aren't special', and what I mean by that is they aren't what you would call 'natural salespeople' (you know the type: high-energy, extroverted, often the centre of attention and full of conversation). If you're a 'natural' like that, awesome: it can be very useful in sales. However, Sarah's gift, I believe, is to work with normal people, many quite naturally introverted, and show them how to sell in a way that fits their personality, their beliefs, and their 'energy' to create highly profitable businesses which lead, eventually, to an abundance of money, time, and freedom.

Most of the issues I come across when I see an expert trying to teach someone how to sell more effectively is they share what's worked for THEM, and they often fall into the high-energy self-promotional type. What Sarah does, and what this book will do if you apply the advice over time, is show you how you can find your own style of sales that works for you, no matter your personality.

I think this is truly game-changing.

I've seen firsthand the power of her work and how she takes normal humans and makes them special, giving them the tools, confidence, and mindset to sell without coming across as sleazy or pushy.

And once you have taken the time to learn and apply what she teaches, it's just down to you to take your genius out into the world and get paid what you're worth, which I think is pretty cool.

In closing, I'll just say that sales and the ability to sell, especially in the current climate (2020), is going to be one of the most valuable skills to master, and with Sarah's direction, your future is going to be bright.

Here's to your future sales success!

INTRODUCTION:

HOW IT CAME TO THIS

I was born into an entrepreneurial family. My parents founded and ran a number of businesses during my childhood, which evolved over time as opportunities arose, from hydraulic engineering to catering. As I got older, I inevitably got sucked into the family business, working full-time during school holidays, and ending up running the businesses solo for a couple of weeks a year to give my parents a much-needed holiday. The hours were gruelling, but the experience taught me so much about business, staff, customer service, and the day-to-day running of a business.

The expectation from the staff and customers was that I would take over the business once I had finished school. Although, not once did my parents place that expectation on me. The natural progression in my family was to head to university, and that was exactly what I did. Very predictably, I went to study business.

I was on a mission: I wanted a decent job with a decent company so I could get a house with 'room for a pony' or, more specifically, my beloved horse. I spent a year on placement as part of my degree and landed a very sought-after role with the confectionary company Mars, supporting the sales team in their coin recognition unit division (the technology in vending machines that knows you've put in a real coin and not just a plastic disc). This was the first time I truly got an insight into what sales involved. The most appealing thing was that the salespeople didn't have to sit in an office all day; instead, they travelled about in their very nice company cars — I was sold!

I returned to university for my final year clear that an office environment was not for me and that the freedom of sales was the best option. I got on another mission, juggling final exams with job interviews so I could go straight from university into my independent life. I secured a job with an international medical-device company, and so my life in medical sales began. Just five days after my final exam, I started on their eight-week residential training course.

This was to be the most comprehensive and valuable start to my sales career I could have wished for. At the time, the commute and the time away was a total inconvenience, but I really didn't know how fortunate I was. Just eight weeks later, having been trained to the point of almost being choreographed, I was good to go.

My initial customer base was district and specialist nurses. On reflection, it was a gentle introduction into the medical world at a time when resources and time were not stretched like they are now. This initial role marked the start of a 12-year career in medical sales (with the exception of a two-year career break to travel the world). I moved from sales representative to account manager, then to key account manager, taking on more responsibility and opportunities to train others. Eventually, I finally landed myself a role as product manager (under the quirkiest of managers I have ever worked for) at a lean but very successful pharmaceutical company based just outside London.

At the same time, Martin (my husband-to-be) and I dabbled in a number of different start-up models. We secured investment in an artisan food subscription box company, marking the start of our life in the online sales world. Whilst the business was found to be unscalable, the lessons, contacts, and business experience we obtained in those two years provided a strong foundation and awareness of the business opportunities that existed online and the challenges and needs that many of those businesses had.

Back at my day job, the company was fantastic and heavily invested in me. I was newly married, and Martin and I made the decision to start a family — something that can really impact your career development. The company was really supportive, but as soon as my daughter arrived, I knew I couldn't continue to give everything to my role and be the parent I wanted to be.

I saw an opportunity in the online world to help those who had a great product offering but had no sales and marketing know-how to do their offering justice. This lack of experience resulted in attracting the wrong sort of clients and making them feel they were barely scraping by. I used my maternity leave to explore this opportunity and set up a sales training business. By the time I needed to hand in my notice, I was generating enough income by working part time to cover my share of the bills. I was also already expecting my second child. My boss was fantastic and tried to persuade me to stay, but my mind was made up. I felt all the emotions at once: I was doing this working-for-yourself thing for real!

Whilst my motivation was lifestyle from the beginning, I was adamant I wanted the business to be a success. It would not be a 'hobby job'; it needed to pay for itself, and pay me. Within 18 months, the business was paying me more than I was taking home in my corporate job. I was confident I could 'tick off' the business as a success in its own right.

To create efficiencies and save us time, Martin and I made the decision to merge the lead-generation agency Martin ran under his name with my sales training business. Using predominantly organic marketing, I increased awareness of the sales element of the business, but our ideal customers were fundamentally different. The sales training attracted customers who should be focusing on getting their message right and securing consistency in their unpaid advertising, while the marketing agency was all about clients who knew their ideal customer and were ready to scale with paid advertising.

At the same time, Selling Without Sleaze as an approach had evolved. Describing pushy sales techniques as 'sleazy' resonated with me and, more importantly, my audience. People could easily understand what I was talking about. Having always been a fan of things 'doing what they say on the tin', it seemed the right time for Selling Without Sleaze to go out on its own.

Similar to the way in which the business has evolved, the programmes and support packages have developed too. It was important I implemented my own advice in the business, so my packages are based around the needs of my ideal customer and will continue to develop as my ideal customer, and my understanding of their needs, change.

Hopefully, as you read this, you have already found similarities between yourself and those whom I enjoy working with. You are great at what you do, but what you do isn't sales and marketing. Some of my favourite clients came to own their own business not because they wanted a business, but because they were passionate about what they do. Running their own business was the only way to do what they did in the way they wanted to do it.

Running a business essentially requires you to do everything: sales, marketing, production, admin, finance, and the list goes on. However, rarely is someone good at everything. Being aware of what you are good at and where your weaknesses lie are the first steps to addressing those shortfalls.

I work with so many people who are on what I call the 'hamster wheel' of implementation. They're busy working hard with a handful of clients, so desperate to develop the business beyond where it is that they have little time to invest in moving it along. Many of them are disheartened by the thought that if they developed the business further, they would not find the time for those additional customers.

Breaking free and taking your business to the next level comes from change. If you only do what you have always done, then you will only get what you have always got. This was a sentiment expressed by Henry Ford, and I think it's totally true.

Most people realise that things need to change when they've become tired and despondent, and fallen out of love with their business. Despite their efforts working in the business, they move no further forward. They're always financially scraping by and working with people who tend to be tricky and demanding, who don't appreciate the value they're getting. Sales is the clear problem because there isn't enough revenue coming in to reinvest in the business or even for the business owner to be financially comfortable.

Are you aware of your competitors performing better than you despite you having a better product offering? This is where marketing and sales can make the difference (even though it shouldn't), and that's where I come in. I'm working with people just like you who want to get in front of better-quality customers and convert them into their ideal customer, so they are earning more and running a business in which they can feel confident.

By the time you finish this book, I would love for you to feel more positive about sales and more confident about what to say and do to get in front of and convert your ideal customer. If nothing else, I hope to change your thought process on the 'sleaziness' of sales! You can sell effectively and successfully without resorting to underhanded (sleazy) sales techniques, and I'd like to talk you through how.

So, if you're ready to get started, I'd like to begin by introducing you to TACC, an acronym that encompasses my simple-to-follow sales framework: Target, Approach, Communicate, Close. With TACC, you can increase your sales, sleaze-free.

1

TACC: TARGET, APPROACH, COMMUNICATE, CLOSE

(WHY SALES IS SO IMPORTANT)

My experience has taught me that with structure comes clarity, which is essential for making that 'thing' happen. When I know what I am supposed to be doing, it is much more likely to get done. I procrastinate less, focus more, and know when to celebrate a job well done — which is, of course, the fun bit!

I must admit that giving my approach the structure and framework it needed took me a lot longer than I thought it would. But that level of clarity was needed if I was going to make my programme as easy as possible for clients to follow and implement. Done correctly, the structure would help more people enjoy the freedom and excitement that comes with selling confidently without feeling like you are being too pushy or sleazy.

Over time, working with so many ideal customers (more on this in Chapter 2) from a range of different backgrounds, my training evolved from the 'sexy sales call' to the overall customer journey. And from there, the acronym TACC evolved, providing me with that clarity and structure I had been looking for. That's when Selling Without Sleaze as a movement was born, and that's what I am sharing with you in this book.

HOW IT ALL STARTED

'The thing is, my competitor's product isn't as good as mine. People who use mine always tell me how great it is, and they are shocked more people don't use it.'

If I had a pound every time I heard this, I would have a lovely passive income! My clients' products/services may vary, and their markets might be totally different, but the feelings of frustration bordering on despair are always the same.

During one of my firstborn's late-night dream feeds, I pondered the reason for this mismatch of clients' skill and popularity. (As those of you with children will know, this is not the feed for cooing and being all inter-active; the aim is to fill them up with milk and get yourself to bed, ideally without totally waking them up. Hence the name the 'dream feed'!) This was a whole new online world to me that, thanks to my husband's business, I was beginning to be exposed to. Up until this point, my sales skills had been mostly reserved for the medical devices and pharmaceu-tical world, with the exception of working in sales for events and festi-vals for our start-up business. This all seemed so entirely different! There seemed to be so many talented business owners out there creating fantastic products who were struggling to generate even a fraction of demand that their product offering seemed to deserve. I spent that feed wondering what it was.

Fast-forward a couple of weeks, and I was looking around a day care for my child. The career woman in me was still adamant I would be heading back to full-time work in nine months' time and being that version of the successful woman who seems to have it all. There was, however, a niggling feeling also at play, making me feel all weird and totally incapable of being more than 10 minutes away from my new little bundle of joy. *These were just hormones,* I kept telling myself, *and they will pass.*

The nursery owner talked me through the lunchtime and teatime structure. She said, 'We sit round a table, just like a family, because for the full-timers, this is the only chance they will get to sit like a family all week.' And with that one sentence, that niggle became an overriding power, and I decided, before I had even finished the nursery tour, that under no circumstances was I returning to my corporate job. I wanted a career, but I wanted those teatimes too, and not just at weekends. So, I began thinking.

As my husband will tell you, 'Sarah on a mission is a force to be reckoned with.' I didn't have the time to mess about. I wanted a new plan for my career, and I wasn't prepared to press the pause button on progressing my own skills and achievements while being a mum. As I drove home, my mind returned to what I believed was that opportunity, that unmet need, which so many business owners seemed to have: effective sales and marketing tools.

Having done more research, I found one significant drawback. The individuals experiencing the 'mismatch' in the quality of their offering and the uptake of it that I had pondered during that night feed were really reluctant to 'do' sales, mostly because they had misconceptions about sales. There was no mistaking my challenge: those misconceptions and reluctance among my potential clients to 'put themselves out there' were significant barriers to overcome.

I thought long and hard about making these people my target audience. They needed to be open to learning new things and selling if I was going to have any hope of helping them and creating myself a business from it. I immersed myself in online networks of businesspeople, joining groups and overhearing Martin talking to clients about their business challenges. After that, I was ready to strike! Or so I thought.

First things first. I knew I needed to test the concept to make sure that I could get results working with these non-corporate businesses, and that they were willing and able to pay for training. Explaining the structure of a sales call came easily to me (I have been using my own version, plucked from the hours of professional sales courses, successfully with customers for years), but what took me by surprise was the absence of true pre-selling prior to these calls. There were high expectations for a sales call, and people were putting pressure on themselves to generate a sale from what was, fundamentally speaking, a cold lead.

I was also beginning to understand the varying abilities of trainers and 'gurus' in the market and the pressure tactics some were employing to get people to sign up to their sales training programmes. It felt so wrong to see how people were encouraged to behave out of character, and so very sad to witness how some customers were being treated. The disciplined and highly regulated industries I had worked in had unwittingly sheltered me from ever being in a position to learn these 'bad' habits. My sales successes, performance awards, and invaluable customer relationships had all been achieved towing a very strict line of conduct. Witnessing the chaos that derived from the 'freedom' of a market that wasn't regulated was inspiring and frightening in equal measure.

The whole premise of the sales process is that you, the seller, get to know the buyer. There are many parallels to dating in this process, and I must warn you in advance you will be subjected to quite a few of them during this book. At this point, I only want to emphasise the need to be considerate of where you, the salesperson, are in relation to your potential customer. For instance, do they know who you are? Do you know who they are? Are you sending information out into the world and hoping it resonates with someone? Or are you focusing on a particular group of people?

I knew after my very first one-to-one session with one of my beta testers that I needed to provide them with a non-corporate, easy-to-follow structure to understand where in the process potential customers were, and what the business needed to do to generate more sales. Following well over 500 hours of sales training later, TACC was born.

WHY TACC?

I created the acronym TACC to help clients understand the steps they need to go through to secure consistent sales. They need to Target, Approach, Communicate, and Close.

As you will learn, 'what', 'where', and 'why' are all fundamental questions that your ideal customer must answer before you can even begin to sell. It's not as sexy or exciting as branding, colour palettes, fonts, and websites; but I promise you, I have seen businesses with all these things who are yet to secure a paying customer. On the other hand, I have seen, time and time again, people generate consistent sales simply by addressing the T of TACC.

So, what does Approach mean? Well, it means approaching your ideal customer confidently with information and messages that resonate with them. This is the beginning of the process of getting them to notice you. This is not like a peacock flashing his feathers, basically screaming, 'NOTICE ME', nor is this about you or your product; it's about your ideal customer, what they are experiencing right now, and understanding what their needs are. Your confidence is a key element in how successful your approach will be. Chapter 4 will go through in detail how to get your head in the right place to make the most of your approach.

Another element of approach includes protecting your business. Putting all that hard work into increasing awareness of what you do only for customers to purchase from your competitors is really disheartening, as is getting onto a call with a customer who has not been pre-sold enough to be in a position to buy from you confidently. That's why the A of TACC includes pre-sale considerations. When you do start communicating with your customer on a one-to-one basis, the groundwork must have been done so that your sales conversation is more effective and efficient!

The first C of TACC, Communicating, covers live communication with your ideal customer on a one-to-one basis. This is what I call a 'sales call'. It can be any live conversation that occurs between you and your ideal customer, which could be over video call, phone, or the traditional in-person sale. It's worth noting that it's easier to communicate the more senses you have available to you. Video calls, for example, are preferable to phone calls, where you have no way to gauge body language.

Whatever the platform, the key thing these calls have in common is that they are 'live' verbal communications, where you need to keep the communication going. There is, therefore, pressure to be able to respond to the customer and keep the momentum going, unlike forms of less personal communication. Live conversations build rapport the fastest and have the highest probability of a positive outcome. That's why they are so valuable, and why it's worth overcoming the pressure associated with this type of communication.

The second C of TACC, Closing, tends to be the bit that everyone gets hung up on. In reality, it's the conclusion of all the hard work you have put in up to now with TAC. Of course, if you haven't done the groundwork right, it isn't going to run so smoothly. I often describe the closing sales call as an exam: by the time you get to the call there is very little you can do other than go through the process; your fate has already been sealed. Yes, you can get it wrong by not putting in the effort required on the closing call, but in the vast majority of cases, the client has already made up their mind based on the information and support provided in the previous three stages.

The Close is about being clear with the next steps and making sure you follow up and deliver on what has been agreed. In essence, if the TAC has been done well, then Closing is the fun part where you can enjoy the fruits of your labour.

Target
Approach
Communicate
Close

TACC IN PRACTICE

Having a structure is invaluable, but without clarity on what you are trying to achieve, you can end up moving, with enviable focus, consistently in totally the wrong direction. That's why one of the very first things I do when I start working with clients is to get them to map out their goals. When we start applying TACC, we then have a goal and direction to keep us on track and ensure resources (both time and money) are spent in the most effective way.

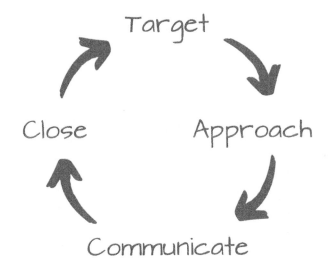

Within your business, TACC is a continuous process for as long as you want to attract customers. You will have multiple customers at various stages in the TACC process at any one time.

From its humble beginnings with five beta clients, TACC has been taught to a wide range of clients (from political consultants to skincare producers). No matter the industry, there is the same consistent factor: they want to generate more demand from the right kind of customer to enable them and their business to reach its full potential.

But there is only a finite amount of time in a day, so I felt it was about time I made TACC more accessible to people. What better way than through a book? My thoughts were that those people feeling trapped on the hamster wheel of implementation, at the expense of their own business growth, can begin moving away from clients who don't appreciate what they do or pay them according to the value they provide. They can use TACC to focus on and work towards the future they want for themselves and their business without me physically being there to assist. Hopefully, along the way I'll be changing some of your minds to reconsider what sales stands for and how you can sell without sleaze.

So, let's get started on the first worksheet: Goals.
Hop over to my website to access the PDF:
www.sellingwithoutsleaze.com/bookresources.

SECTION I:

TARGET

2

WHO IS YOUR IDEAL CUSTOMER

(AND WHAT DO THEY NEED)?

I must warn you in advance, the ideal customer is one of my most favourite topics! I spend a significant amount of my time talking through and referring back to clients' ideal customers. The information gleaned from understanding your ideal customer forms the basis of and feeds into many aspects of TACC and decisions you make around your sales, marketing, product development, and even business direction.

WHO IS YOUR IDEAL CUSTOMER?

Lots of people get hung up on the idea of focusing on a specific person or group of people. This creates a real mental block. I'll be going into this below, but for now I just want to emphasise that this approach will help you attract people you want to work with. It's not designed as a repellent or a way of alienating or excluding people.

Your ideal customer might not be any of the customers you are currently working with. To be honest, most of the businesses, when I start working with them, aren't working with their ideal customer. Most of them don't have a clear understanding of who their ideal customer is but know it's not who they are working with right now!

Put simply, your ideal customer is a bit like your dream partner (yes, back to the dating analogy again!). If you could create your dream customer, who would they be, what would they do, and what characteristics would they have? This could be based on a dream client you previously had or someone imaginary you hope exists.

As we work through this chapter, you will see that the information you have on them could be based on fact, assumptions, or total guesses. This can sometimes feel as if you just plucked something out of thin air, causing you to feel disheartened about the value of the exercise. However, please do me (and yourself) a favour and stick with it. The work will help, I promise.

I first met Holly because I was interested in using her services. I was about 10 kg overweight and unhappy with how I looked, especially as this coincided with creating videos and 'putting myself out there' more. The issue was that I love my food and don't want to eat less of the fun stuff. I literally wanted to have my cake and to eat it, too.

Holly was recommended to me by my business mentor, and I organised a call. To be fair, her sales conversation wasn't too bad. She clearly hated talking price and was charging about a third of what she should be charging. However, as a potential customer, it was clear to me it was a bargain. At the end of the call, I mentioned what I did and how I help people target their ideal customer and charge prices that reflect the value they provide.

We ended up organising another call so she could find out more about what I did. During that, it became apparent that Holly wasn't working with her ideal customer at the moment. She had been running her business for over four years by the time we met. Her clients were either super demanding or totally unmotivated. Like so many people I start working with, Holly was clear about who she no longer wanted to work with, but less clear about who her ideal customer really was.

Sometimes, knowing what you don't want can be as enlightening as knowing what you do. Knowing who Holly's ideal customer was not, this was the first thing we focused on. After years of struggling financially and to achieve a work-life balance, her substandard business/clients had really taken over her life. Things needed to change.

SIX QUESTIONS TO ASK YOURSELF

Like Holly, you need to start with what you know. If you have a 'champion' customer you enjoy working with, who got great results and still raves about your product or service, then that is great and a fantastic starting point. For others, you might never have met your elusive ideal customer, but you hope that special someone is out there. Alternatively, like many of my clients, you might know you have a group of current clients who are definitely not ideal; people with whom you wouldn't choose to work. In fact, the thought of going to work fills you with dread!

When I get a client on board, the first thing they do is work through their ideal customer — it really is the foundation for your sales and marketing. You will find in the worksheet at the end of this chapter six questions that will give you a starting point to understand your ideal customer better. These questions are designed to encourage you to question what you do and don't know about your ideal customer.

You need answers to all the questions so you have a complete picture. Sometimes, gaps in your knowledge can be plugged by doing a little research. Other times, you need to go with your best guess. When this is the case, I make a note that the 'facts' are based more on guesswork than reality. I would, therefore, expect to be updating these answers as further information is obtained.

The key thing to remember, is that, like in any relationship, your understanding of who your ideal customer is and what motivates them will evolve. No love story has a happily ever after ending: there are periods of both understanding and disagreement as you navigate relationships. The relationship evolves and changes based on different internal and external factors. And that's exactly the same as your ideal customer.

It is important to accept that things will change. Keep yourself up to date by staying closely in touch with your ideal customers and be sure to obtain information from more than one source. What I mean by this is that it is easy to become close to one or two of your customers; it is very easy to think that they are the norm and that their outlooks and opinions are a reflection of what all your ideal customers are thinking or doing. In fact, other ideal customers are experiencing totally different scenarios and challenges. The best way to safeguard against this is to be aware of the size of the sample of customers you are basing decisions and changes on.

DO I REALLY NEED AN IDEAL CUSTOMER?

Yes, you really do! Why wouldn't you want to resonate with and, thus, attract clients you really want to work with? This has to be the single biggest area of resistance when I start working with people. There is a genuine fear of missing out, excluding customer groups, and missing out on much-wanted sales.

I don't EVER turn people away because they don't fit my ideal customer profile. I have no checklist of exclusions that dictates 'If you don't tick half the boxes, you aren't coming in.' Rather, your ideal customer profile should be used as a guide so that your messaging speaks to the people you can best serve. My ideal customer tends to have a more gentle, less forceful style of communicating, which is often associated with women. That doesn't mean that I don't work with men; in fact, around 35 percent of my clients are men. It just means the message I communicate tends to resonate more with women because I am talking to them and creating content and imagery that appeals more to them.

When targeting your message, you will always attract people who are what I call the 'peripheral' ideal customer. These are the people you wouldn't expect to attract but something in your messaging is resonating with them. Depending how far removed from your ideal they are, it might be worth checking if you are a good fit, if you will be working with them on a one-to-one basis. If you sell more products, there's less of a need to check the fit, but it is worth being clear on the features and benefits of the product to ensure it is what they expected. The key thing here is that you aren't going to turn them away just because they don't fit the ideal customer mould.

Use the information you create in your ideal customer profile effectively and you can create your dream working conditions, having an impact on clients you enjoy serving, and who have the means to pay you what you want to be paid in return for the value you provide.

WHY KNOWING YOUR IDEAL CUSTOMER IS ESSENTIAL FOR BUSINESS

I keep saying that knowing your ideal customer provides the foundations for your business, so I thought it only right to talk through exactly what that means.

Let's return to Holly's story. Once Holly determined who her ideal customers were, she was able to figure out where she might be able to find them. This was based on knowing what their interests were and where they hung out on social media. Not only did that make getting in front of her ideal customer easier, it also made it possible to prioritise the promotional platforms Holly needed to use. This immediately saved her time and meant that she could produce better content. Therefore, she was able to have more of an impact on the platforms where her ideal customers were most active.

How did she know which platforms they were present on? Once we worked through what her ideal customer was like, it became apparent that Holly had worked with people before who were close to but didn't exactly match her ideal customer. She, therefore, found out from those past customers their interests and social media preferences.

Even if she hadn't yet encountered a near-ideal customer, she could have used clues from the profile she had created for her ideal customer to understand where they were likely to hang out. This would, of course, have been an assumption, so the work that she would need to do on each platform would have to be a test. Nevertheless, it would have still provided a starting point. For example, if your ideal customer is quite sociable and aged between 35 and 45, they are likely to be active on Facebook or Instagram.

Once we figured out where they were, it was important we determined what style of communication they preferred, what style of communication Holly generally gravitated towards, and what words and messages did or did not resonate. A big part of this approach involved looking at where Holly had managed to attract customers who were close to her ideal, and then working from there on how the process—specifically, the words and messages used—could be tweaked to enable her to find her ideal customer. There was, again, an element of trial and error, but it was a lot more focused and targeted than a stab in the dark.

Key messages to communicate to your ideal customer can be found by understanding what is going on in their life, what their current concerns or sources of happiness are, what their priorities are, and what their motivations are for using what you provide. All of these pieces of data help you build a clear map of what to and what not to say. Without this information, it is easy for your messaging to miss the mark and not resonate with your ideal customer.

For example, when COVID-19 hit in the UK and the government announced a lockdown, Holly's ideal customer's main concern was no longer about improving their health or performance. It was entirely focused on helping their business survive. If she had continued with the original messaging planned for that timeframe, she would have been totally out of sync with what was going on in her ideal customer's world. Because she stayed aware of their changing situation, she was able to adapt her messaging to resonate with her ideal customer in their new circumstances. Despite the uncertainty in the market created by this change, she was able to have her best month ever in April, six weeks after the lockdown began.

IDEAL CUSTOMERS ARE PAYING CUSTOMERS!

Like many business owners, Holly found that the people who needed her help the most were the people who could least afford her ... this isn't news to a sales trainer, let me tell you! The most in-need business owners I come across are those who can't afford me. By sheer nature of what I do, I meet so many people who — with only a few simple changes to their sales process — could make their businesses considerably more profitable. However, that information has value and shouldn't be given away for free because if that person will profit from it, why shouldn't you? It's a real-world example of needing to secure your own oxygen mask first.

Is your ideal customer someone who cannot afford to pay you? The answer is, of course, no. Additionally, people who are paying you what they perceive to be a large amount of money for your services tend to be the most demanding and difficult to deal with — again not making them ideal.

For those who aren't in a financial position to use my services, I have a paid 15-minute 'business accelerator' option. I charge a minimal amount of money for the session, which comes with a guarantee that if I can't help them with their business challenges, I will give them a refund. They need to provide information in advance of the session, and then we work through (in most cases) the best way to generate income. This gives the clients a starting point, but if they also go away and action the suggestions, they could easily see a reason to invest further in my services using the money they have generated. For this reason, I also provide free insights, hints, and tips on my social media channels to help people start making changes in their business.

For me, this is a satisfactory solution to meet the needs of those who cannot yet afford me. I know from experience that supporting people on a basic level does convert them into paying customers later, and prevents others paying a lot of money only to discover their concept doesn't have legs. Unless you run your business as a charity, you need to protect the value you provide. If you don't protect and value what you do, nobody else will.

Head over to my website to download the
ideal customer PDF worksheet:
www.sellingwithoutsleaze.com/bookresources.

3

UNIQUELY YOU

(POSITIONING YOURSELF IN A CROWDED MARKET)

In the last chapter, we looked at your ideal customer, who they are, and an overview of the elements of their profile that can help you steer your marketing, sales, and even business goals in the right direction. If you took one thing from Chapter 2, I hope it was the fact that it is essential to get to know your ideal customer if you want to make it as easy as possible for yourself to sell without the sleaze.

In this chapter, we will be exploring the importance of also getting to know your market and competition, warts and all. This understanding means having a clear picture of where your strengths lie, what your potential weaknesses are, and the risks that exist in the market. The thought of these things can be very daunting, especially when starting out; most people would rather focus on the opportunities that exist. I can totally relate to that, having been there with my business. But in reality, you can prepare, plan, or take preventative action on things you aren't aware of.

The best thing you can do to futureproof your business is to face up to the reality of what is going on around you and decide on a course of action based on the information available.

As Sir Francis Bacon said, 'Knowledge is power.' This is particularly true when it comes to understanding your market and competition. Honestly, you can't know too much. Of course, saying that, I just want to clarify that there is no point in getting transfixed on your competition and following what they do move for move; you need to create your own path and do things the way you would do them because no two businesses are the same. But, keeping a healthy awareness of what competitors and other players within the market are up to can help keep you relevant.

FOCUS ON YOUR MARKET: A WARNING

'We have created something totally unique that our customers really want; we are going to kill it in the food subscription market.' I remember uttering words to this effect at an investors' meeting. My husband and I were confident and excited to be moving forwards with our concept: a subscription box where you select the products you want to try from a themed shortlist every month. We were the only ones who offered this flexibility. We had listened to our ideal customers and addressed the biggest drawback of the competition. Looking back on this naivety now, I shudder. We didn't do enough research around others in the market, and what was going on in the market as a whole. We focused our attention on our ideal customers but didn't investigate why competitors might not be fully meeting our ideal customers' needs.

The main comfort I take from this experience is the fact that I have since managed to stop so many others from making a similar mistake in their market, urging them to look around and see WHY others aren't meeting a glaringly obvious need before investing more money in their business. In the excitement of a new product or discovery, it is so easy to get carried away. Cognitive bias sets in and you only look for evidence that validates your idea, making you overlook information that goes against or contradicts it.

As with your knowledge of your ideal customer, you really can't be too informed about what's going on in your market. Starting off with the basics, it will hopefully come as no surprise that you need to understand who your direct competition is and what they offer in comparison to you. Looking into what is being said by the competition can be really enlightening; the messaging your competitor is putting out will be directly influencing what your ideal customer prioritises.

For example, when I worked in the medical devices market in the UK, I sold a silver dressing designed to kill bacteria in infected wounds. The focus of all the companies in the market was around the quantity of silver needed to kill common bacteria. Our dressing contained more than the others, so we pushed the need for a high level of silver to be present in the dressings to ensure bacteria were killed and didn't become resistant. To counter this argument, competitors moved to talk through the 'potential' (unsubstantiated by direct evidence) impact of too much silver in a wound on healing rates. Whilst unsubstantiated, this suggestion had enough logic to it that customers began to question what the optimal level really was and how much was too much.

The company I worked for was very efficient at keeping communication channels open between the marketing team (which set the message) and the sales team (which was on the ground, finding out what competitors were saying and doing). The company was, therefore, able to respond quickly to counterclaims competitors were making about the product. Had we been less efficient or aware of competitor claims, this would have had a negative impact on sales. The longer a competitor pushes a particular message, the more set in stone people's opinions about it become, making it much trickier to sell against.

As I have touched on with the medical example, it is essential to understand what your strengths are and how you measure up to your competition. Where do you beat your competition hands down, and vice versa? Why are they, or you, so much better? What stops that from being replicated? Everyone has strengths and weaknesses; what are yours?

KNOW YOUR USPs

I regularly meet business owners who are struggling to pin down their unique selling points (USPs). Often, these business owners are in saturated markets where, by their own admittance, they are 'very much of a muchness.' This must not be the case. If you can't explain to a potential customer why they should use you over a competitor, you are never going to convince people to use you. If you can't convince them that you are the best person to meet their needs, you will always struggle to attract customers.

Albert Einstein once said, 'Everybody is a genius. But if you judge a fish by its ability to climb a tree, it will live its whole life believing that it is stupid.' For me, this quote really captures why it is so important you understand where your strengths are and maximise them. Your strongest USP in the majority of cases is *you*, so you need to be making the most of your unique skills and experiences.

But what if you are reading this book and want to be an expert in something that you currently lack the necessary skills and experience in? I definitely won't tell you not to bother. However, I will suggest that you don't give up your day job to jump into a market where you can't provide valuable USPs. You will need to assess the market, understand where the gaps in your skills and knowledge are, and work to plug them until you are *as good* as your competitors in some aspects and *better than* in others. Otherwise, you will be like someone attempting to win a marathon with minimal training against athletes who have been running them for years.

Value to your ideal customer is the currency we are really talking about when we discuss USPs. It's all well and good saying you have 30 years' experience in the market. But if that experience has no value if it doesn't equate to results, more insights, better techniques, or judgement that will help customers achieve things faster, experience better results, or enjoy a superior experience. USPs need to relate to what the customer wants or needs. This is what will get customers choosing to use you, or your product, over your competitors.

There are ways to encourage customers to prioritise your USPs, especially if you firmly believe that what you are saying is true and in the customer's best interests to understand (as in the silver dressing example).

Educating your ideal customer can be a fantastic way to build trust in you and your offering.

HOW DO YOU MEASURE UP?

Understanding where you measure up in comparison to your competitors enables you to understand:

- what your USPs are

- where your weaknesses are

- how to set your price

The questions at the end of this chapter will prompt you to think about the value you provide in comparison to your competition. Being aware of your wider, indirect competition and what they are up to is also important. Your ideal customer has finite resources (time, people, or money) available to them. They, therefore, need to prioritise how they allocate these resources. My rule for understanding your direct and indirect competition is to look at two things:

1. How closely what they claim to provide matches what you claim to provide

2. How closely your ideal customer matches theirs

Your direct competition claims to offer the same outcome (benefits) as you. Your indirect competition, whilst much less of a threat, will exist in the same market as you but, although offering a different outcome, will still be targeting the same people. Your indirect competitors are often businesses you could end up partnering with in a joint venture, referring your non-ideal customers to (and receiving referrals from), and collaborating with. These indirect competitors are influencing factors in your market and potential sources of distraction. Therefore, they are always worth keeping an eye on and building connections with, unless they complement what you do and encourage customers to progress onto using your service.

You should be mindful of the fact they can negatively impact your sales if, for example, they are running sales or offers that could boost spending in their area of the market and reducing interest and demand in yours. Taking matters one step further, there is always the potential that these organisations, once they have built up their customer base, could look to expand into other areas of the market and start offering services that compete directly with yours. Whilst this shouldn't keep you awake at night, it is worth keeping up to date with their activities and being aware of how you can protect your business.

It's also essential to understand where you fit within your market as far as your ideal customers' trust and loyalty are concerned. How aware of you are your customers? How aware are they of your competition? What are their perceptions of both you and your competitors?

Audiences both online and offline are a valuable resource and currency. If your competitor is more highly regarded than you by your ideal customer, take note and work on your message. I can't mention this without warning you that it is better to sell yourself on your own merits than to go down the route of discrediting others or selling yourself based on their shortcomings. You can highlight differences in customer service, for example, by sharing your own great reviews rather than talking about the lack of quality service others provide.

DETERMINING YOUR PRICE

The value you provide should directly relate to your price. This is where we went so wrong with the food subscription box. We positioned ourselves at the same price as our competition whilst providing so much more value. When looking at where we were in comparison to our competitors, we should have positioned our pricing higher.

If we had looked into the logistical implications of customers being able to choose products for their box, we may have decided — like our competitors — that it wasn't worthwhile offering customers that opportunity. Instead, we could have competed with our competitors on customer experience.

If you provide a service but don't have the experience and, therefore, can't give the same value to your ideal customer as your competitors, then it makes sense to be charging less for your service. But it only makes sense until such time as you are providing equal value, or even better, AND have the testimonials/evidence to back that up.

However, if your skills and knowledge put you in a unique position to support your ideal customer and give them value way beyond the competition, it would make sense to charge more. There is a slight caveat with this. Your ideal customer will have a level at which they might not be able to afford you, in which case you can choose to go after another sector of the market and an ideal customer who *can* afford your pricing. Or you could look to scale down what you offer and lower the price; for example, providing less product or a one-to-many (group) format for your service.

You also need to consider that price is a filter. Sometimes you can price yourself too low, causing your ideal customer to question the value they are securing at that low price. I always use one of two analogies to describe this. When asking clients which one I should include in my book, the votes were pretty 50/50, so I'm going to use them both.

A. The Parachute Jump

You have to do a parachute jump. There are two parachutes for sale. One costs £5, the other £200. Which one do you choose? I have only ever had one person say the £5 one, and he was a base jumper who knows how to pack and check a parachute. Literally everyone else chooses the £200 option.

Why? Because they don't know what they don't know about packing and making a parachute function. When you get to this stage (which is normally why you pay someone else to do something), you just want to make sure that you have done enough to ensure a positive outcome.

B. The Boob Job

The second example I use, mostly with women, is buying a boob job. If you were to go through the effort of having a boob job, would you choose the £50 option or the £3,000 option? Fundamentally, some things aren't worth opting for the discount! Just like the parachute, you want to ensure the most positive outcome possible. An operation isn't something you want to repeat because you went cheap the first time. When you are looking for aesthetic improvement, the extra money is worth it for the peace of mind that the finished product will be what you hoped for.

In both cases, I hope it's clear that having a lower price actually deters customers. I have worked with clients who, due to predominantly moral drivers, have chosen to go with a 'fair' price rather than the inflated prices their markets have created. In this case, it is essential to educate your ideal customer and be prepared to call out the competition for charging more unnecessarily if you intend to gain enough trust from your ideal customer.

Price can also work as a client filter. Charging a higher price tends to filter out clients who are likely to be less experienced and, therefore, more demanding. The most difficult customers in our lead-generation agency have all been at a lower price point. Their businesses are less successful, in most cases because their product is weaker or they are just starting out, and the investment is more of a stretch for them. These are the clients that tend to turn into nightmares because they *need* a return on their investment.

Compare this to a client who can afford you because they have a successful product, which is generating them enough money to afford to branch out on their marketing. They have the systems in place to handle the enquiries because they already have a decent demand. They already know the value of marketing, because they have seen the impact it can have. They are much more organised, professional to work with, and aren't overstretching themselves to work with you. Which one would you prefer to work with?

WHAT IF YOU DON'T KNOW YOUR MARKET ENOUGH?

We secured investor funding with our food subscription box, helping us create the website we needed to test our concept more fully (still with a customer focus but also taking into consideration efficiencies). At the price we had decided to charge, we were a no-brainer in comparison to our competition. We figured we would be able to scale well once we had nailed our marketing and cost of customer acquisition (how much it costs us to attract and secure a customer).

We were pleased with our progress, and so were our investors. The problem was, as we grew, wastage didn't come down; in fact, it increased. Food producers who supplied us with the products demanded items be ordered by the case or box, which meant we would have surplus. Despite scaling up, some less popular product lines still had low demand from customers. We got to the point that producers weren't able to fulfil larger orders within the agreed timescales — or they wouldn't provide them at the price we had originally agreed.

On reflection, there had been warning signs of this. Producers themselves told us nightmare stories of our competition screaming down the phone for more product, or to get orders out on time, or bullying them into accepting a lower price. We had naively put this down to the bad reputation our competitor had and didn't delve further for more information; we just took it at face value. Had we investigated, it might have revealed the challenges around getting producers to stick to their agreed pricing, volumes, and timescales, and the viability of us providing the service at such a low price.

We had also totally overlooked a significant number of suppliers. By nature of the menu element to the box, we needed to work with a diverse number to change up the options every month. We also needed them to be 'lifestyle' business with little, if any, aspiration to grow. Those that grew quickly ended up on supermarket shelves, which meant they no longer met our artisanal criteria.

Had we been more aware of these factors, our ideal-customer market research would have focused on a different price point. As we later found out, this would have indicated that fewer customers would be willing to pay the higher price needed to make the product viable. Our indirect competitors were supermarkets, which all compete on price, and making customers increasingly sensitive to cost. Charging £4.50 for homemade jam when people could buy a decent brand in the supermarket for less than half that was a challenging sell.

The only comfort we took from making the very sad decision to cease trading was our investors' response. Whilst we had failed, we had done so quickly and learned a lot. In my mind, we didn't learn as quickly as I'd have liked, but we had apparently been a whole year ahead of where the investors would have expected us to be, based on the volume of testing we had done with different routes to market, marketing approaches, and troubleshooting. From a financial perspective, despite a considerable amount of personal debt, we had saved ourselves another year of wasted financial investment, which was a small consolation. A friend reminded me of the quote attributed to Will Smith: 'Fail early, fail often, fail forward.' We had failed early, and we had learned so much in the process.

Running that business for 18 months taught me more than four years at university studying business. Failing early (and as cheaply as possible), appreciating the need for research to understand the entire market, and experiencing the business process from start to finish were all things you cannot learn in theory in a lecture theatre. The lessons I learned have also added value to so many of my clients, and my audience, and for that I am grateful. Even though it cost me four times what university did, the learnings were far in excess.

Knowing where you fit into your market and the value you bring has a massive impact on your self-confidence when it comes to approaching your ideal customer. We will be exploring this together in the next chapter, but first, complete the competitor analysis worksheet: PDF available at **www.sellingwithoutsleaze.com/bookresources.**

SECTION II:

APPROACH

4

INNER BELIEF

(PREPARING TO APPROACH)

In the previous chapter, when I shared my start-up experience with our subscription box company, there was a lot of talk around failing. Sadly, 'failing' carries a lot of negative connotations. It's painful, so I get why you would want to avoid it. But there is much that can be learned from it. Honestly, failure is a learning experience, and the only time I find failing a waste of time or a source of frustration is when a mistake is repeated (and this is because I am someone who likes to be efficient). I tend to get aggravated when I feel the lesson could and should have been learnt the first time.

Franklin D Roosevelt said, 'A smooth sea never made a skilled sailor.' It's one of my favourite quotes because it supports my opinion that the difficult times can teach us the most. I wouldn't be much of a sales and business mentor if I had never run a business or if I had never messed up making a sale, or had never secured a sale, for that matter. Mentoring for me is all about working with someone who has been there, done that, and made the costly mistakes so I can learn from their experiences (learning that comes at a fraction of the cost and in a significantly shorter amount of time).

But what has all this got to do with approaching your ideal customer? Well, I want you to think about the worst-case scenario — 'failing' in a call — and see it as a learning opportunity, rather than a reason to throw in the towel. And I'm hoping this will provide the first step to getting your head in the right place to be the most effective salesperson you can be.

Whilst it is possible you can talk yourself out of a sale during one customer interaction, there are so many more potential customers out there. It really isn't the end of the world if you end up in that worst-case scenario, but what is more likely is that you simply won't do the best job of convincing your ideal customer that you are the answer to their problems, and everyone will leave feeling a bit flat, potentially confused, and uninspired. However, you can come back from that; I have seen it happen.

THE IMPACT OF MINDSET

As Babe Ruth would say (here comes another lovely quote), you should 'never let the fear of striking out keep you from playing the game.' I find this is particularly true when it comes to selling. If as a business owner you shy away from selling, not only will you be missing out, your business will also directly suffer. So, what can you do? Well, let me tell you about a very talented lady called Phoebe.

'Looking at my account,' Phoebe confessed, 'I have the money for the first instalment, but I'm not sure where the other two instalments are going to come from. I know I need to do something, and I think your course will help, but I just want to be honest with you.'

I could tell that she was being genuine, and that her business was in a very tricky situation. This wasn't the conversation I had been hoping for, but I knew if she was prepared to implement what we discussed on the course and work hard, we could turn things around.

We were six weeks into lockdown in the UK, thanks to a frightening number of COVID-19 cases. Businesses had been hit hard, and Phoebe's was one of them. Overnight, whole industries had literally ground to a halt. Phoebe helped creative businesses secure funding. Whilst I understood that direct sources of funding had disappeared for Phoebe's customer base within days — and therefore demand for her services — there were things she could do, and needed to do, if her business would continue to exist.

The weight of responsibility of continuing for the sake of her staff was really heavy for Phoebe. She felt terrible. There was so much talk in her market about the lack of opportunities to generate money, and staff were being put on furlough. Not only did she feel bad, her income was also drying up. Phoebe was hearing from clients almost daily that they could no longer pay their creative talent's retainers, would need to pause their retainers, or were going to close.

In the short time that we had during our initial call, as an outsider looking in, I felt that there were opportunities to provide support (paid support, at that) to her ideal customer. We just needed to investigate what that support looked like. If nothing else, people were aimless, confused, and unsure about the future. Addressing one or more of those elements in a paid workshop or presentation would more than likely generate income. However, I believed we had better resources — they just needed uncovering.

CHANGING YOUR PERSPECTIVE

During our first session, we examined where Phoebe's business was and, most importantly, what was happening for her ideal customer. In this scenario, things had changed for them overnight. Whilst she had kept in contact with clients, their outlook, and that of the wider industry, which is quite close-knit, was all about what they could no longer do and what the future held.

It was very doom and gloom, but Phoebe was too close to it all to see a different perspective. The group learning environment of my Sales Academy, which she had signed up for, was exactly what she needed. Hearing about what other businesses were doing to pivot in their markets was a great source of inspiration to focus her attention on.

I challenged Phoebe's view that there was nothing her ideal client could be doing. We discussed talking through the shortfalls in knowledge prior to lockdown; how unprepared clients were to apply for funding;

the need to get applications for funding right if they wanted to secure any; how things were going to get even more competitive; how windows of opportunity, when they did open, would be shorter. I felt we were definitely getting somewhere on this new thought process.

One of the best things you can do is to step outside of your 'normal' and get a different angle on things. But how does this all relate to your sales? Well, in the same way as Phoebe wasn't questioning her business normal, she wasn't encouraging her customers to think outside the box either. I regularly need to encourage customers to be the 'ray of sunshine' in their customers' days — not the source of more pain and misery!

Until Phoebe was in a better headspace — i.e., seeing opportunities instead of the doom and gloom — she had no chance of convincing anyone to part with resources. Once she reframed this in her head as an opportunity to get ahead, be prepared, and make the most of lockdown, she was in a position to sell that to her clients.

Within three weeks, Phoebe had created the structure for, marketed, and launched a training course, helping clients to get their strategy sorted. When funding opportunities did appear, clients would be ready to apply and get their applications in, despite shorter timescales. Her clients would be more effective and efficient, so that they were much more likely to secure funding in a more competitive environment. The course sold out in four days. In fact, she already had a waiting list for the next one, which she didn't even have a date for yet!

KEY MINDSET AREAS

There are three main mindset areas that affect your effectiveness with customers:

1. Your belief in the impact you can have on a client.

2. Your confidence and passion — in yourself, your offering, and what you know.

3. Your ability to deal with knockbacks.

These are the three most important areas to get right in order to get out of your own way and be as effective as possible at sales. If one or more of these needs working on, it is well worth taking the time to address it. Get yourself in the right place to do yourself and your business justice.

1. Belief

Regardless of whether you are selling a product or service, if you are not hand-on-heart convinced that you are the best solution for that person, it is very difficult to sell to them.

Have you ever tried convincing someone that something is a good idea when you don't actually believe it yourself? Maybe it was a friend who is having doubts about marrying their partner you never liked in the first place. It's impossible, isn't it? Well, it's the same in sales.

If you are reading this book thinking, *Actually, I think there are better things out there for my ideal customer than what I have to offer*, then you really do need to take a look at yourself and why you are selling what you sell. Of course, there are going to be potential customers you speak to who aren't your ideal customer and better suited to another solution. However, I'm talking here about your ideal customer as a collective.

Disillusionment often comes when you work for someone else. I have been there myself. Taking a job based on the information you can gather about a company and its products is a big leap of faith. It stands to reason that you can get it wrong, and you can't be passionate about the product or the product area or you're left selling the 'white elephant' in their product range.

If you find yourself selling something you aren't passionate about, don't quit on the spot. Review the situation and ask, is there scope to change your mind? Can you get more into it? Can it help you figure out what you will enjoy selling? I can guarantee that even if you take a cut in basic salary to change industries, with the right commission structure in place, you will end up earning more selling a product you are passionate about.

If you sell your own product or service and are struggling to reignite the passion for what you sell, then it's time to take stock of where you are and why you are doing it. What made you lose that enthusiasm? If you genuinely feel there are better options out there, what are you going to do about it? What do you need to bridge the gap and make yourself a competitive alternative? I have spoken to many people at these crossroads. Some have really turned it around; others have chosen to just walk away. Out of those who I am still in touch with (which is most of them), none have regretted the choice they have made. You need to do what is right for you.

What about if you are just having a wobble? We all have a crisis of confidence from time to time. Having covered the worst-case scenarios earlier in this section, hopefully you are thinking along the lines of, *I am struggling to get in front of customers but feel confident about what I do*; that is totally normal. There is a certain level of vulnerability when it comes to putting yourself out there and selling what you believe in — especially something as close to home as a product/service you have designed and created. It's easy to take feedback personally, and in the sometimes-lonely world of running your own business, it is easy to lose perspective on feedback or let it have more of an impact than is healthy.

If you're struggling to believe, first of all, it's good to explore why. Was it a specific incident? An accumulation of a number of incidents? Has it crept up over time or have you always felt this way?

Once you can figure out the origin of behaviours or feelings, they often lose their power, allowing you to gain a new perspective and take back control over how you are feeling. A really useful exercise to do is to collate evidence of the impact you have had on a client. David Goggins, in his book *Can't Hurt Me* (2020, Lioncrest), talks about a figurative cookie jar that contains a selection of achievements from his life that he can dip into when the going gets tough and self-doubt creeps in. He metaphorically reaches for the cookie jar and picks out a fact about himself to boost his confidence and give himself the belief that he can do anything. I love this concept, and I have seen it work really well over the years, personally and with clients.

There is no denying the facts about what you have done to help others achieve or experience. Having these facts as a reference, ideally noted down, is a very powerful way to get you into the right mindset to appreciate the value you bring. When I work with clients to recognise their value, the barriers they had around what they charge for their service/product totally disappear; it is very empowering.

Whether you are providing a product or service, you are only responsible for your share of the outcome. When things don't go to plan and you receive negative feedback, or people don't get the results they are looking for, it is worth taking time to review the part you played, what you can do differently next time (if anything), and what was outside of your control. It is very easy to dwell on the negatives, but that won't help you get out there and help people who want to be, and can be, helped by your product or service.

2. Confidence & Passion

If you don't love your product or service, nobody else will: fact. In order to do your offering justice, you need to share your passion for it.

Along with passion, you need to know your stuff when it comes to your market and who your product or service is for. Gone are the days when you could hold all the information on what you and your competitors do. Information is readily available on the internet for everyone, and your ideal customer will be confused and overwhelmed, unable to fully understand all the facts and information available to them. With this shift in access to information has come a change in your role in the decision-making process: you are expected to be the expert, to know more than Google on your subject and, most significantly, be able to help the customer understand which information is important and which they can disregard so that they can, with your help, make an informed decision. It is more important than ever before to be up to speed and to be an 'expert' in your field if you are to provide the best sales experience to your ideal customer.

With knowledge, proper planning, and preparation comes confidence. So many of my clients turn around their mindset on the sale process purely by practicing and expanding their sales toolkit. This kit comprises their go-to phrases, examples, and explanations for their sales conversations. Over time, you will see the same questions, objections, and concerns being raised by your ideal customer. Knowing that you are able to address them succinctly and effectively enables you to feel more confident when communicating with customers and allows your passion for your area of expertise to shine through.

Passion and confidence are contagious. When someone comes across as bored or insecure, it can make the customer question why: is it that you are nervous? Or is it that you aren't convinced about what you are selling? Don't make your customer question your confidence in your product offering: make sure that you know your stuff.

3. Coping with Knockbacks

However good your product or service is, you are going to experience rejection. It's part of the sales process and, although easier said than done, it shouldn't be taken to heart. Try to remember that there may be a lot going on for your potential customer that you aren't privy to, from personal challenges to busy workloads, and now might genuinely not be a good time for them to invest in what you have to offer.

Being able to keep perspective when you experience a 'no' is a useful skill to master, and a number of things can help you to do this. One way is to 'hedge your bets'. Particularly with high-value ticket sales, it is easy to focus all your attention on that one big opportunity. Then, when it doesn't come to fruition, you are starting again from scratch. So, make sure you keep your sales pipeline well stocked. This will take some time management skills on your part, but it will be well worth it to help you maintain momentum when an opportunity doesn't come through for you.

Another coping strategy is to know your numbers. If you know what your conversion rates are, it helps you to keep in perspective all the opportunities that come to fruition and those that don't. For instance, if you know that for every five booked calls you have, you will convert one caller into a paying customer, it makes sense that you will hear four nos — that's just how it goes. I am not saying, however, that you shouldn't review your calls for what went well, what didn't go so well, and what you would do differently next time — every customer interaction is a learning opportunity. But using that information to change your future calls, rather than dwelling on four failures, is the most constructive thing to do.

You only fail when you make exactly the same mistake twice. Any other time, a mistake is an opportunity to learn and improve; they should be used in a constructive way to help you increase your effectiveness and serve your ideal customer better. 'Beating yourself up' about them won't help anyone.

BE THE RAY OF SUNSHINE

Phoebe had become 'the ray of sunshine' in her market for her customers. She was selling them hope at a time when everyone was telling them there was nothing they could do. Her genuine belief that she could help them, as well as her sense of urgency that they should get on with it now, was contagious.

If you were caught in a storm and had to abandon ship, would you rather be in a lifeboat with someone who believes you can't make a difference and should just surrender to the inevitable, or someone who wants to take action and save themself? That's exactly who Phoebe was becoming for some of her customers: the person who could help them work through and find solutions. That's exactly who she wanted to be for them.

To back it up, Phoebe was also achieving results with her customers. With those testimonials and increased enquiries came opportunities to bring staff back to work, and even take on new members of the team to support the increase in demand. Through the feedback, testimonials, and evidence of the impact she was having, Phoebe felt so much more confident about the value she provided to her customers. I have a lovely caption from a Zoom call with her where she rips up a note of her ideal pricing structure. Today, her prices are so much higher because she understands the value her customers get and her true financial value.

Phoebe's programme provided her clients an opportunity to get organised ahead of funding streams opening. This helped her ideal customers, who were motivated individuals within the market, to help themselves. Just being present and proactive in the market provided Phoebe so many speaking opportunities — all of which she now gets paid for. Companies are approaching her for all different kinds of work within her field, from creating courses for their members to writing applications on their behalf.

Her main business problem has changed from keeping her business afloat to taking on the right new staff to support the business's growth.

Phoebe's story shows that showing up for your ideal customers during the difficult times creates a lot of value. Not only has it elevated Phoebe's reputation, and that of her business, during a difficult time, she also positioned herself as a reliable partner. She didn't disappear when her ideal customers lacked direction, panicked over their own business future, and were unsure of what to do. Instead, Phoebe stepped up and guided — something that will be remembered and rewarded with loyalty by her ideal customers. And all because she chose to do something instead of nothing and get her head in the right place to best serve her customers. Now Phoebe and I are working on protecting her business and the brand she has created — something we are going to be looking at in the next chapter.

Before that, get yourself in the right mindset by working through this chapter's PDF worksheet, available at **www.sellingwithoutsleaze.com/bookresources**.

5

MARK YOUR TERRITORY

(CREATING THE RIGHT OFFER)

Securing your business isn't just about finding customers now; it's also about putting your 'stake in the ground' and being clear what you specialise in, who you help, and what you stand for, both now and in the future.

The best way is to keep these things in mind from the beginning. I have worked with a number of people who haven't thought twice about protecting their business in the long term until a competitor shows up — by which time all the low-effort, high-efficacy ways of protection are out of the question. This is when concern can quickly turn to panic. So, if securing your business — both from competitor and market positioning point of view — hasn't been on your radar so far, tune in and start making those small changes that add up now.

Suzanne came to me as a referral from a previous client. The person who referred her has always been vocal about the impact I had on her business and was someone who had attended a workshop I ran. Suzanne, therefore, came very pre-sold and eager to get results, so she signed up for the Six Weeks to Start Up programme, extending it by another six weeks so we could continue to work on her business development. From the outset, we knew there was a lot to cover.

Suzanne was a very smart lady. She had a degree in architecture, a post-grad degree in anthropology, and had spent a lot of time in the academic world. Her specialism was urban planning and design. The challenging thing about academics, civil servants, and healthcare professionals in the UK is that they don't knowingly sell anything in their day-to-day work. The securing of their service is totally detached from their daily activity; therefore, not only can sales and marketing seem alien, it simply doesn't appear on their radar and doesn't get prioritised. Whilst this isn't a problem in the healthcare setting (people can get on with doing what they are good at), it is a major issue from a business perspective. If you find yourself in this situation while setting up your own business, don't panic. It's not a reason to not run your own business; it's simply something to be mindful of. Ensure you take the necessary training or get the right support to get yourself up to speed and accountable when it comes to prioritising your sales and marketing.

Suzanne came to me because she was looking for help with generating an income with her urban planning and design skills. She had secured a number of 'conversations' with relevant company departments and applied for jobs but had gotten nowhere. Most people valued her unique skill sets but struggled to see how that fitted within their organisation. She was having to do a 'double sell' (I'll cover that in the next chapter) without the clarity of knowing exactly what she was offering or to whom.

She knew that people needed her skills, because other countries recognised the need to apply social impact studies to urban developments. The absence of knowledge when it came to social impact is what prompted Suzanne to leave her architecture job in the first place and return to studying. Without the awareness of social impact in a development, Suzanne felt ill-equipped to design something that would last and serve the community it was for. Her biggest challenge was communicating this to the right people — that's what we needed to work on.

She didn't mind if the logical step was to set up her own business, seek employment, or return to the safety of the academic world — which understood and welcomed her value. What she needed was clarity and a plan. This wasn't my usual ideal start-up client, but based on the initial information she gave me — plus her preference to pursue a career outside of academia — I felt I could help her go down the employment or start-up route, both of which are fundamentally about sales. I told her I would be able to help her reach her goal, but if I couldn't, I would give her a refund — nothing ventured, nothing gained!

Now, at this stage, Suzanne was nowhere near being in a position to create an 'offer'. She had no idea what she could provide or, more significantly, who her ideal customer was and what they wanted. Further investigation and research were needed to determine what gap she filled.

CREATING A VIABLE OFFER

If you don't have a decent offer, it's not going to be worth the effort of protecting, nor is it going to be easy to protect. So, we are starting from the beginning: the creation of your offer.

What is an offer? It's a product or service that you can sell to your ideal customer — or to anyone, in fact! For services, it normally takes the structure of a pre-prepared programme or resource. For a product, it's a physical item, designed in most cases for a specific use. Having something already created should make it easier for your ideal customer to buy from you — as long as it's what they actually want! There are two ways to design an offer: (1) based on your own assessment of need or (2) based on the needs of a specific audience whom you consult with along the way.

Consultation is by far my preferred method, but 90 percent of people I work with come to me with an offer in place and need help targeting customers who would benefit most from it. Any offering not created via consultation is unlikely to tick all the boxes. Think about the times you have needed to consult your other half, close friend, or relative about their birthday present because you wanted to get it right. You know this person really well but weren't confident enough to take the plunge and buy them that gift. So, why do it with your ideal customer?

I appreciate you are probably sitting with my book with an offer already created. For that reason, I will move on and stop talking about *why* you should do it and start talking about *how*. Next time, though, please do keep in mind that the best way is to use your ideal customers to help create the solution that they are looking for.

The Reality of Your Offer

For those who want to revamp their offer or look to create a new one, the best place to start is with the need that you are trying to address. For Suzanne, it was the need to create urban developments that not only looked good but also served the community long term. She, therefore, appealed best to ethical developers who were faced with more challenging planning applications, where they had to take into consideration social impact and integration of the development in the wider community. This didn't mean every development was her target, but there were more than sufficient developers to keep her busy and support her revenue goals.

Analysing Your Offer

It's always good to assess the potential drawbacks of your solution. Suzanne was aware that her skills wouldn't be valued by all developers unless they were forced to show more social awareness. But by working through the various stages that would fully utilise her skills on a project, it was clear there was a further drawback: she couldn't do it alone. There were elements that would need to be provided by third parties, meaning that she would direct a team, rather than provide the whole solution herself.

Moving on to look at the wider market, it is always important to look at the barriers to entry for direct competition. In the UK, there had been little emphasis on social impact studies among developers, but there was increasing pressure for this to be included with planning applications and project proposals. This meant that it was a perfect time for Suzanne to push her services; meeting this emerging need was a great opportunity. Equally, it would be a great opportunity for others, so both Suzanne and I were keen to ensure that she protected her 'space' in the growing market for the long term. In order to do that, we worked through a system of analysis that she had created and patented the process so that it couldn't be replicated, thereby creating a significant barrier to entry for other potential competitors.

I encouraged Suzanne to continue networking with different people in her market. She was fantastic at using her connections but just needed to be smarter about where she spent her time and with whom. Was there scope to do business or was it really just a social thing? Even asking this basic question got her thinking and prioritising her time. The more practice she had at talking about what she did, the clearer and more succinct she got, and the easier it was for people to understand her value.

People understanding your value and being willing to pay for what you have to offer are completely different things. One drawback that became apparent early on with Suzanne was the timing of her approach to potential customers. She provided a service like no other, but still needed to be part of a wider team in order to have a tangible impact on a project. With that in mind, we looked at who she should be approaching as her ideal customer. It made sense for that to be individual project managers who provide the skilled contractors for a development (the architects, surveyors, planning advisors, and so on), rather than the developers. She can be provided as part of a package, and companies could use her skills as a USP for their services — a nice add-on to enable projects to 'tick the box' in their development project application.

Suzanne was beginning to find her place in the market, carving out her own position. Approaching this ideal customer worked, and Suzanne was quickly included in pitches and contract discussions: she had her foot in the door.

SECURING YOUR 'SPACE'

It's not enough to sell the solution; you need to sell why you are best placed to provide that solution. Without this, you run the risk of convincing someone that your solution is the right one, only to have them head off with that solution and choose your competitor instead of you. This is super important, even if you currently have no competition. This feeds into the 'double sell' explanation coming up in Chapter 6.

Working with Suzanne to identify where we could secure her position and offer, we decided upon a series of lectures. This would position her as the go-to for social impact in urban design, and it was a popular subject, welcomed by the industry, as well as academics. She was at last able to make the most of the gap between the academic world and practitioners looking for real-world insights. She quickly became known by colleagues, and more requests for presentations and lectures began to trickle in.

Finally, we looked at exactly what we offered her ideal customers. Suzanne was very ethically and morally driven, and whilst she would find others who shared this outlook, she would have more of an impact and generate more demand for her services if she spoke her ideal customers' language. If she didn't resonate with them and their priorities, someone else would: she needed to talk more business if she was going to secure her space.

Now, as I have said in this chapter, people from healthcare and education backgrounds don't have sales and marketing on their radar. This is where the networking really helped Suzanne out. We explored what her ideal customers' priorities were, not just in terms of the people who supplied skilled personnel but also those who were involved in the contracting and tendering process. If she was going to be included in a project, she had to talk the right legal and technical language, and demonstrate how she could help them achieve their goals. In doing this, she would differentiate herself and secure the testimonials she needed to secure her USP.

We set to work determining what motivated the various stakeholders in the decision-making process. If you are dealing with a range of stakeholders, you often need to address their needs and motivations separately if you are going to get them all on board. We identified two key stages where she was most likely to get a result (it always makes sense to go for the easy wins first and branch out from there). We focused on the different motivations at each of these stages, and language used by these stakeholders. Suzanne quickly secured meetings with them, because her message resonated with them. She was on the way to securing her offer, and her first paying client too!

We used the principles outlined in the last chapter to determine the value she was providing versus other options out there and decided upon a day rate that she felt comfortable with. In no time (only eleven weeks), she had her first paying client. With a clear understanding of what her ideal customer wanted, a clear framework for helping them achieve that, and a reliable pricing structure, Suzanne was set up to replicate what she had done to secure her first paying client.

With each happy client comes a testimonial that will provide further social proof and evidence of your skills and value, strengthening your position in the market and setting you apart from the competition. In Suzanne's case, with her unusual mix of academic qualifications, experience, and IP, she now has had a very secure position in her area of the market.

If that sounds appealing, then start securing your niche right now by working through the worksheet for this chapter, available at ***www.sellingwithoutsleaze.com/bookresources****.*
Remember, knowledge is power: once you know where your weaknesses are, you can work to address them.

6

PRE-SELLING

(TAILORING YOUR APPROACH FOR YOUR CUSTOMER)

In the last chapter, I talked about the importance of securing your product both in the minds of your customers now and for the future. By factoring this in when creating your offer, you make your approach so much easier. Another element that often gets forgotten in the heat of the chase (yes, sales really can get that exciting!) is the pre-sell, which is the warming up of a lead in order to make the sales call your grand finale (or, as I like to describe it, the 'exam bit' of the sales process).

Why wouldn't you want to make things as easy as possible for both you and your customer? If you tailor your approach based on your ideal customer and their needs, you are much more likely to convert them into a paying customer. A tailored approach saves you time and money while helping your ideal customer make the right decision quickly. So, let's jump into what pre-selling looks like and how you can use it.

WHAT IS PRE-SELLING?

Pre-selling is the process of helping your ideal customer to get to know, like, and trust you enough to buy from you. This tends to be in the form of content and resources, and generally not in the form of live interaction (that's a sales call, which will be covered in the next chapter). People tend to need to get to know, like, and trust you before they will commit to buying from you, especially when there is a big resource commitment involved. When I say 'resource commitment', this tends to be time or money.

I once bought a sponge via Facebook. It came in a pack of two and cost less than £2. I checked out the comments on the ad, clicked through to a reasonably decent landing page, and ordered it. The time and financial commitment were so negligible that I didn't need to do much research.

In comparison, when we were looking for a mentor to help us with our lead-generation business, the investment was in excess of £15,000, and we would be working alongside that person for a year, on a one-to-one basis. We took more than three months making a decision to hire someone. We had multiple phone calls with his salesperson, as well as the mentor himself, and we ended up taking a short course with him before upgrading to mentoring. Simply because the stakes were high, we wanted to be sure we were making the right decision.

Keeping this in mind, it makes sense to tailor your pre-sell based on the level of commitment you are looking for from your customer. A video call with the CEO would be total overkill for the purchase of a sponge. Equally, straight to a landing page for a service costing £15,000 wouldn't get you many conversions. It's all about the sort of content that you put out to your ideal customer — we will come onto that — but the top line is you need to tailor it based on your ideal customer and the stage they are at in the customer journey.

WHAT HAPPENS IF YOU DON'T PRE-SELL?

Natalie was a great client to work with. She ran a programme to help people manage anxiety. She was a real action-taker who took feedback really well. When we first started working together, she was spending excessive amounts of time (over an hour) on each initial free consultation with people who had no intention or means of purchasing her product. Things had to change.

Now, I am a big advocate of using organic marketing to establish a clear understanding of your ideal customer. When I say 'organic', I mean attracting leads using free content on social media platforms and growing your audience by making new connections, sharing your expertise for free, and leveraging other people's audiences. To be clear, this is totally unpaid. The reason for this is you are paying for the leads using your time rather than your money, and you are learning about your ideal customer in the process.

The most successful clients in the agency have come to us with a clear understanding of their ideal customer, informed by the organic way in which they have grown and nurtured their audience. Additionally, a product that has done well organically has a proven track record of demand (proof of concept, if you like), in comparison to an untested product, which requires you to start testing audiences and messages from scratch.

Natalie had been sucked in by the simplicity of Facebook ads and mini funnels to drive traffic. Potential leads would join an email list in return for a 'lead magnet' (in this case, a short, actionable resource that enabled them to see how effective her methods could be and help develop trust in her). Or for those leads keen to get started, joining would allow them to book a consultation call. She was running very low-budget ads (costing less than £10 per day) for this funnel and was securing occasional calls.

The quality of these calls was poor, which led Natalie to seek help. Her conversion rates were poor too, and the time she spent on these calls was unsustainable. Her product cost close to £1,000, so the need for a call was borderline. It was only worth it if she had the right pre-sell game and had built up her audience.

As it stood, she was a faceless name behind a paid advertising campaign that went into a reasonable email sequence. There was a lot of encourage-ment to book a call but no compelling reason for a discerning, genuine customer to book one. Instead, she was left talking predominantly to the lonely and those that wanted to 'offload' rather than those who wanted to make a change in their lives. The work that needed to be done was clear, so we got started.

FEED THE NEED

If there is one question about your ideal customer that is essential above all others it is the question of need. Without this knowledge, you can work through all the elements of TACC, but your level of success will always be limited. This can't be a best guess; you need to know exactly why your ideal customer would buy what you have to offer.

In the scenario with Natalie, as we looked at her most successful clients, it became apparent that her product wasn't for just anyone with anxiety; it was someone who had social anxiety but who also *genuinely* wanted to help themselves get better. This latter part was a real revelation and game changer. It meant that Natalie could tailor her content to attract those who truly wanted to make a change — not just anyone with the condition. Within this market there were a lot of people whose sense of identity was interwoven with their condition, which resulted in some who (subconsciously) didn't want to get better — these were definitely not ideal customers for Natalie. Not only would she be more invested than them in making a change, they would also be more high maintenance and much less likely to achieve good results.

You want to be attracting your *ideal* customer in your pre-selling approach. It is too easy to get caught up in just attracting anyone. I have seen time and time again the outcome of this with people coming to me with mediocre results, tricky clients, a low price point, and a business that keeps them busy without any hope of timeout from the hamster wheel. These people are burned out and disillusioned with their business and desperate for some decent revenue and an opportunity to get some work-life balance back.

So, how do you find out what they need? Communication is key. Understanding what is happening for them, what they are experiencing, and what they want to do about it are all great starting points. The best way to find out is to spend time with your ideal customer. Back in my medical sales days, I spent time with all my key customers, understanding their role and the pressures they experienced. To be honest, it was something that the company encouraged. I must admit I was less than enthusiastic to start with — I didn't find wounds that exciting!

There was no denying how beneficial that time with the clinicians was, though. As it turned out, our competitors didn't do it. It was a great way to build rapport and to understand more about their role and the type of work they did. I still have strong memories (and in some cases nightmares!) about what I got to see, but it enabled me to understand, and the customer to feel understood. Both are very powerful outcomes.

You might not be in a position to shadow your ideal customer for a day without appearing a little strange, but there's nothing wrong with a quick coffee or taking them out for lunch in return for picking their brains. Most people feel flattered to have their opinion asked for. However, it is worth noting that you need to spend time with more than one of your ideal customers in order to determine what is truly going on.

The important thing when looking at each of your ideal customers' needs is to figure out what is driving it. For example, with Natalie's clients, there was normally a specific event or occurrence that acted as a catalyst. This was either something that made them think enough was enough, or a landmark situation that was coming up (like a family event) that meant they felt compelled to 'get things sorted.'

Before we started working together, when Natalie did her initial call, people would say, 'I have had enough', or something along those lines, and she would move on in the conversation using that information. This insight wasn't enough for Natalie to truly sell her solution; she needed to understand the emotion behind that statement and action. Why not sooner? Why not later? Why now?

Once she got an understanding of the driving force (emotional element) behind that need, it was much easier to sell to that person. Emotions are a big part of the buying process; that's why so many people make spontaneous purchases only to regret them later when the emotion has receded. Tapping into that emotional driver makes selling much easier, because it enables the customer to understand exactly how you can help them whilst making them feel understood.

Often when people are selling, they use leading questions with potential customers, such as: 'Would it be useful to be able to be in a social setting and feel confident?' Now, most people would agree that it would be useful, but the person asking the question is still none-the-wiser as to whether this is a priority for the customer — or, if it is, where it fits into their world. What might be a more effective way of asking clients is using open-ended questions such as:

- How important is it to you?

- How much does this impact you?

- In relation to other priorities in your life, where does this fit?

- Is this change a nice-to-have or a need-to-have?

All the above can provide a sense of perspective about your ideal customers' priorities. Remember: this is all market research. You should be using current or past clients for this stage so that you aren't selling; you are researching. These phrases can and should be used in the sales process — but fight the urge to approach colder potential customers with these questions.

Finally, it's important to understand the pace at which your ideal customer makes decisions, and what information they need before they feel in a position to make that decision. If your customers have a pressing need, their decision-making process is likely to be short. If, on the other hand, they are in no hurry, you may need to provide a justification or incentive to get them moving through the process quicker.

Your ideal customer is likely to be someone who doesn't take an age to make a decision. And if those who take a bit longer to decide end up being the loyal customers getting the best results, then a longer decision-making process could be a small price to pay. That's why it's important to really get to know your customer and understand what makes them tick. Providing them with the information they need to make a decision and progress along the sales process can help your ideal customer feel ready to buy sooner.

WHAT IS YOUR SOLUTION?

Where does your solution fit with your customers' needs? It is essential you understand where your solution ticks all the boxes and where it falls short. This can sometimes feel like a harsh reality check, but without looking at these things, you will struggle to predict the risk factors, prioritise the value you provide, and sell against competitor strengths.

Is your solution mutually beneficial? For example, I have worked with a number of personal trainers who, in pursuit of work-life balance, have wanted to take their personal training online. Freeing themselves up so they are no longer on the gym floor every evening and weekend is their priority. But it provides no advantages to regular clients unless the trainer is well known and in high demand, or the customer doesn't need the face-to-face time with a trainer — but this is why most people use them! This has resulted in a number of people offering the same sort of remote programmes without first creating the results they need to establish a reputation for themselves.

I'm not saying they shouldn't change their business to make it work for them. After all, why work for yourself if you can't make your life easier? But it's essential to keep in mind that if you do something like this, you are in effect creating a drawback to your services by changing them to work for you rather than your customer, which you will need to explain in calls.

Take the opportunity to have a serious look at your business and solution to see how and where they fit in the market. Once you are clear on your solution, you can make changes for the long term and approach the ideal customer.

HOW TO USE THIS INFORMATION TO 'APPROACH'

It was obvious when we started working with Natalie that she needed to work more at her ideal customer's pace. Getting clients to book a call and then be in a position to sign up to an £800 programme was a steep ask. So, how did they want to be sold to?

We needed to figure out the best way to make contact with the leads coming through from the ads that Natalie was running. Her customer base was naturally introverted and private, so a group setting would likely be too quiet with few interactions. Utilising her email list she compiled with addresses of everyone who downloaded her free resource was the logical option.

We also revisited the resource that was on offer. If Natalie wanted to attract those who wanted to make a change in their lives, the offer needed to appeal specifically to them. It made sense to change the resource to one that appealed more to those who wanted to take action immediately. She also needed to be clearer with her message and opinions when communicating with her email list. This would mean people who weren't action-takers would unsubscribe from her email list, but it makes sense to keep your email list 'clean' with only people who are interested in what you do (especially because you pay higher fees for longer lists).

This was a mental block for Natalie that took time to overcome, and I could totally relate. I too had been resistant to using my opinions as a filter; you can feel quite vulnerable. However, informing and enabling people to know, like, and trust you via email — even encouraging them to interact using questions to create engagement — can go a long way to pre-selling your ideal customer. Pre-selling based on why you are the solution, how you understand the customer, and the impact that you have (be that with a product or service) helps strengthen your positioning, which is what we talked through in the last chapter. It really is an effective use of your time and resources.

Incorporating pre-selling into her approach enabled Natalie to generate more call bookings that converted into a higher percentage into paying customers. As an added bonus, she enjoyed the calls more. They were easier and resulted more often in a sale — what wasn't there to like? Clients were more familiar with what she did, and some were even informed about the cost of her services, leaving her to relax and have a proper chat.

THE 'DOUBLE SELL'

I've touched on double selling a couple of times already in this book, but what is it? A double sell is when you not only have to convince your ideal customer they need the solution you are providing but also that your solution (rather than those available through competitors and other sources) is right for their needs.

An example of this is one of my clients who works in nutrition. She educates people on the value of focusing on their nutrition rather than just hitting the gym to lose weight and feel better. Only when they buy into that belief is there any point in trying to sell them the nutritional support programme.

Being aware of a double sell is important so you can understand how much selling you need to do. It is also vital to remember both sells when you are first to market or have a new concept. You might have the market to yourself for a while; but you will get competitors if the market is attractive enough to investors. If you have only sold the concept and not why you are the best option to deliver it, you have paved the way for your competition to come in and take business from you, even though you've done all the groundwork to make the sale happen.

Do you and your business a favour! If you need to sell the concept of what you do *and* why you are best to deliver it, ensure you do that routinely. Never skip the 'why me' element. That way, if and when a competitor enters your area of the market, you will have already been creating barriers for them by raising customer awareness of how good you are and what makes you best placed to help meet the customer's need. This circles back to securing your business discussed in Chapter 5.

Worksheet time! Download the PDF and answer the provided questions to form the basis of your pre-selling approach. Find it at **www.sellingwithoutsleaze.com/bookresources**.

SECTION III:

COMMUNICATE

7

SALES CALL SUCCESS

(THE SECRET'S IN THE STRUCTURE)

Most people seek out my services for this section of the sales process because the sales call is the area that people can most easily identify as where things go wrong. The call ends, but they haven't secured a new customer for their product or service, and they have that sinking feeling that things didn't go to plan. It was all a bit awkward and uncomfortable.

In reality, as I've said previously, the sales call is like an exam. By the time you get to the one-to-one communication element of TACC, your fate is mostly sealed. You could have the best exam technique in the world, but if you haven't revised and don't know the answers, your technique is wasted. That's why the vast majority of people I work with start right at the beginning of TACC. More often than not, this is where their sales call challenges originate. Around 70 percent of failures are caused by either a lack of customer or market knowledge. For 25 percent, it's their offer or an inconsistent message. Only around 5 percent of people I work with have everything in place, but the sales call lets them down.

CREATING A CALL STRUCTURE

Lauren was one of that 5 percent. Mindset played a significant role in her not being effective in a sales call. Whilst addressing her mindset, self-confidence was also important, plus the fact that Lauren's calls were crying out for structure. More often than not they resulted in a 'nice chat', but no business was completed; the customer was left to 'go away and think about it.'

Listening in to some of the calls was my first step; I wanted to hear what was happening. (Here's a tip: recording your calls is a great way of helping yourself improve. It's really painful to listen back to them but worthwhile, I promise.) Talking through her call preparation, Lauren admitted that she didn't create any goals for her calls. The problem with this is that when you lack direction and you are the one who is supposed to be controlling communication, the call ends up lacking structure. Your customer has come to you to find out more about what you do; they are looking to you to guide them through the sales process.

Having a clear structure to work within for your call isn't designed to restrict you. It's not something you have to stick rigidly to, but it's a fantastic starting point. With structure comes a clear direction and improved experience for the client. By taking control of the call, you're in the driving seat, and you can manage the pace and the direction of the conversation. Therefore, you're much more likely to achieve the desired outcome, and your customer will have a much better experience. At the end of the day, it is your responsibility to guide them through the sales process — you are, after all, the expert.

We are aiming for a call structure that clearly addresses all the elements you want to cover in the time available and yet is flexible: an agenda that you don't share out loud but keep in mind throughout the call. Without the 'flexible' bit, you run the risk of being too focused on structure and not responding to what the customer wants to talk about — resulting in you overcooking it and becoming robotic and unnatural.

It's about striking a balance. Obviously, you need to be listening to your customer. You need to be aware of what people are saying, and you need to be responding accordingly. Equally, you want to have a structure in mind so that you don't end up all over the place and discussing things that are not remotely relevant. The key thing is remaining flexible to what the customer is saying, as you would in a normal conversation with someone in your personal life.

Don't be that annoying person who doesn't listen or appear to care. We've all been in a position when a person asks, 'How's your day?' but, as you begin to reply, it is clear they are uninterested in how your day really was. Their agenda was to be nice and polite — a tick-box exercise. So, if you can't be bothered responding to that person's answer, why ask the question? Exactly the same thing applies when talking to your customer. You'll be asking questions, finding out information about your customer, and it might go in a different direction than the one you're anticipating. The point is, you can bring it back on track, and you can refocus when it is relevant to the conversation.

You are an adult (or a very advanced child, if you're reading this book) who is able to communicate on a regular basis with people. You're able to show empathy and understanding. When you are talking to someone, you are able to ask questions to get clarity. On a sales call, you're using all those elements; you're just trying to put it together in a more structured way so that you can still be yourself AND generate the results you are looking for. That might sound like a lot of things to tie together into one communication, but don't worry! In this chapter, I am going to walk you through it.

THE SALES STRUCTURE

The biggest impact we could have on Lauren's conversions was to provide her with a call structure and clear goals going into the call (more about that later). This made the sales structure as memorable as possible. To help others accomplish this result, I've created the following acronym: SALES, which I will begin to elaborate on in the next chapter.

State
Ask
Learn
Explain
Steps

I use SALES to structure all my sales calls and teach clients to do the same. I classify any conversation which happens in real time as a 'call', be it in person, by phone, or via video conference because all types of sales calls have very similar qualities. They are conversations happening in real time which need to be sustained. You can't disappear to get more information; you have a very short period of time to respond, and you need to keep the conversation flowing. The SALES structure, therefore, is very simple — I didn't want to make it complicated. I want your attention to be on the customer and what the customer is saying, so you can respond accordingly.

The impact on Lauren's calls was instant. Just feeling more in control gave her the confidence to take charge and steer the conversation to keep it on track. This ensured there was enough time to cover all the aspects she needed to, enabling the potential customer to be more informed and have the knowledge they needed to make a decision. Her in-call closes increased — she even managed to start taking card payments at the end.

WHEN YOU DON'T HAVE A GOAL

The phrase 'proper preparation and planning prevents poor performance' is well known because it's right. If you have no idea what you want to get out of a call, you are unlikely to get the most out of it or perform to the best of your ability. It's increasingly difficult to get in front of your ideal customer, so you need to make the most of every opportunity.

Proper preparation means setting yourself up to be as effective as possible. Otherwise, you run the risk of missing out on sales opportunities. If that person wants to buy and you don't make it as easy as possible for them to do so, someone else will! Plus, stumbling aimlessly through a sales call isn't exactly the best experience for your customer. What impression do you want to make?

Calls without a goal in mind tend to go off on tangents, lack focus on the important elements, and result in momentum being lost. There must be a focus on understanding and uncovering the customers' needs because, without an understanding of what they are, you will end up listing features and benefits in the hope that something sticks. This can be a very painful way to sell and often results in a no-sale — especially if there hasn't been enough time set aside within the call to talk through unique selling points (USPs) and provide clarity on the value provided versus the costs incurred.

It's easy to lose enthusiasm for sales calls if they are not well planned. You shy away from making the sales calls your business needs you to make; your sales suffer; revenue drops until you need to refocus your attention back onto calls you don't enjoy — and you would rather be doing anything else. This was the outcome for Lauren.

So, how do you turn it around? It's an easy fix, thankfully.

Before you start a call, take a few moments to think through what you want to get out of it. I get clients to put their call goals into three scenarios: best case, medium case, and worst case. You, of course, aim for the best case, but normally you get the medium case, and that's okay — progress is progress. Nevertheless, the best case will always be worth aiming for. It gives you something to focus on, something you can consider during the call — where are you versus where you want to be? Then, you can get it back on track if it's lost direction.

Now, with a clear goal in mind, you simply relate it to your sales structure to create the 'plan' you need to achieve your goals. Think through each section (this will be your homework at the end of the next chapter), and then it's a case of implementing and tweaking. This process is never complete; there are always things you can do to be more effective in your calls so you can achieve your best-case scenario more frequently.

With all the talk of goals and structure, I don't want you to lose sight of what you are aiming to achieve. As I continue pointing out, the sales process, especially the one-to-one element of a sales call, is just like dating. It is an opportunity to get to know your ideal customer and understand what makes them tick and what they are looking for. The 'fit' needs to work both ways; there's no point signing up to work with a client you can't stand. Keeping this in mind, it makes sense to check in with yourself about how you feel about the customer and play out what it might be like to work with them prior to pushing for a sale — after which it becomes much more awkward to step away.

DON'T BE TOO HELPFUL!

Another client in a similar situation to that of Lauren was Kathy, one of my first clients. On paper, she should have had a waiting list for her services. She was well known and respected both by fellow clinicians and customers, and yet she was struggling to generate enough income to pay her bills. Why? Because she gave away far too much value in the call and was not retaining her focus on the point of the call. By the end, the potential customer had received the equivalent of a full counselling session.

Kathy was effectively meeting her clients' short-term need on that first call, which was to feel much better. The emotional driver for the call — the fact that they felt overwhelmed not knowing what they don't know — had been addressed and their confidence had been restored. Not only was this feeling temporary for the potential customers — meaning, their long-term need hadn't been met — it also cost Kathy sales.

So, what did we do? The solution was simple to understand, but Kathy found it a challenge at first to follow. She needed to be structured in her call and have a clear goal to aim for. We worked through her worst, medium, and best-case scenarios for her initial calls. Once we had goals in place, we worked on the structure and what she would be looking to do and say at each stage in the structure (which we will go through in Chapter 8). It was then a case of practicing.

Kathy had a steady flow of enquiries, but we were both reluctant to practice on potential customers — especially as her cashflow was so tight. Instead, we used part of our sessions to roleplay her calls. Roleplaying with a friend or colleague is often underrated. Working through what you would say in your head just isn't the same. Until you hear it coming out of your mouth, it's very difficult to know how it comes across and make the necessary tweaks until you are happy with your sales patter. A couple of hours of practice can make a world of difference to your sales conversations and how well they flow.

For Kathy, her biggest challenge was not jumping in and trying to solve everything. We ended up creating a list of areas to cover and those to avoid so she was super clear on when she needed to stop talking and get the call back on track. Progress took longer than the overnight shift with Lauren, but Kathy kept practicing with her partner too. Within a couple of weeks, she began to notice an increase in conversions. Within six weeks, her conversion rate had doubled. Talking through the changes, she admitted that she still had to consciously keep the call on track and steer herself away from problem-solving, but it was getting easier. Indeed, long-term habits can be hard to break.

Soon after getting their sales conversions sorted, both Lauren and Kathy increased their prices. In both cases, the increase in price had no impact on their conversion rate — something that tends to concern people when raising their prices. Having successful calls builds your confidence, making it easier to talk price and ask for a fairer return on the value you provide. However, it's always best to sort out your sales process before making adjustments to price. If you aren't successfully converting enquiries, there's no point in increasing, as it's likely to put yourself under more pressure, which is counterproductive to doing well in the sales call.

Hopefully, in this chapter, I have convinced you that having a goal for the call and a structure you can use to achieve that goal are vital and can have a massive impact on your conversion rates. Utilising these concepts means using your time as effectively as possible and generating more sales.

In the next chapter, I will walk you step by step through the first section of a call: taking control and information gathering. But before then, it's time to do your worksheet and get clear on those goals. Find the PDF at ***www.sellingwithoutsleaze.com/bookresources.***

8

TAKING CONTROL

(INFORMATION GATHERING AND LISTENING)

In Chapter 7, I introduced a basic call outline. I use the acronym SALES to structure all my sales calls and teach clients to do the same, and it looks like this:

State

Ask

Learn

Explain

Steps

Now, I'll work through the first section of that call with you step by step, using practical examples wherever possible to enable you to understand how you might use the structure to be more effective and confident in calls. This isn't designed to be a rigid routine you need to stick to at all costs; it's designed as a framework for you to refer to in order to get the most out of your calls. The key thing in a sales call isn't that you adhere strictly to the structure; it's that you listen and respond to what your customer is saying. My structure can help to keep you organised so you can worry less about what to say/do next in order to truly listen.

I first spoke to Tina, a weight loss coach, after she had been referred to me by a colleague. She was a super friendly and approachable person who was loved by her customers — her testimonials were fantastic. In addition to her challenges of attracting enough potential customers onto calls (lead generation), she also struggled with her conversions once she had them on the call. As we talked through her usual call structure, it became apparent where things weren't going so well. The calls were lasting too long, so the momentum was being lost, and the previous training she had received around what to do in a sales call had left her behaving too robotically. She wasn't injecting any of her personality into the call — and her character was the very thing her customers loved the most about her. She was using someone else's words and approach, much of which seemed totally against who she was and what she stood for.

We chatted through how she felt about the current call structure and some of the questions she asked her potential customers. Tina admitted she didn't feel at all comfortable and actually felt really bad for focusing so much on how bad things were and how negatively they felt about themselves. When I asked why she did it, her response was, 'Well, that's what I have been told to do, and I need the sales.'

You should never ever say or do anything in your business that you don't feel comfortable doing. If it's not what you would say or do in front of a friend, don't do it. However effective it is, it's someone else's words and techniques and so it's not authentic. Never ask a question just for the sake of it — your customer's (and your) time is valuable, so use it wisely. Ultimately, you don't want to attract someone else's customers; you want to attract your own. The best way to do that is to be you.

Throughout this chapter I've provided outlines and examples, but you need to adapt them to suit your own character and the needs of your ideal customer.

S = STATE THE REASON FOR THE CALL

In my SALES structure, S is for stating. One of the only things you have complete control of in the call is the opening statement. A bit like providing an overview or agenda, this is your opportunity to let your customer know your intentions for the call. They might have a very different idea of what they want to cover, so letting them know your thoughts is a great starting point.

Sometimes, a call may have been arranged a while ago. The client might have forgotten about it, or they might have a different agenda or something new they want to discuss. If you're speaking to someone who's already an existing customer, they might have other things they want to talk to you about. Therefore, your opening statement ensures you're both on the same page.

The approaches and tools I talk through in this book are there as a reference point. Particularly in the early days, when you are nervous and less practiced, you are likely to refer to them a lot. Over time, stating the reason for the call becomes second nature, but until then I suggest you have two or three versions available to you that you slot specific details into. In your own words, you need to cover the following elements in your opening gambit:

- Who you are (unless you've already been introduced)
- Why you are calling
- The value to them of having the conversation (benefits to the customer)
- Length of time the call/meeting is likely to take
- Check whether what you have just said is okay with them

Most of Tina's customers came to her as a result of a five-day weight-loss challenge, so the goals of the call and the amount of pre-selling was very similar for all of them. We repeatedly practiced the following phrase (we didn't do the intro, as they were already familiar with her due to being in the challenge, so that would have been weird!):

> *The reason for today's session is to look at where you are now*
> *and where you would like to get to with your weight loss.*
> [Why you are calling]
>
> *I can give you an indication of how long you can expect it*
> *to take to get to your goal weight in a sustainable way, and*
> *we can assess if you are suitable for one of my programmes*
> *if you feel you need the support.*
> [Value to the customer of taking the call]
>
> *This chat should last around 15 to 20 minutes.*
> [Length of call]
>
> *How does that all sound?*
> [Permission to proceed]

The value was the clarity about if they were suitable for one of the programmes. We used 15 to 20 minutes as a timescale because if the person wasn't engaged in the conversation, that's how long the call would likely last. But if the person you are talking to contributes to the call running longer, that's a good thing — although you should be looking to bring initial calls for products or services in under the 30-minute mark whenever possible. Finally, it's always important to check that the structure is okay with the customer, giving them an opportunity to raise anything else if they want to.

Now, it is worth noting that sales calls can totally change direction when you ask, 'Is that okay?' It could be due to the fact the person has a specific problem, or they weren't expecting to speak to you about that subject. It could be because that the person is really looking forward to talking to you and already has 100 questions for you. Checking if it's okay with them is their opportunity to raise anything else for you to address without any distraction during the call. You don't want them to be on the edge of their seat, desperate to ask you a question; you want them to be concentrating and in a position to converse with you without distraction.

This first step of stating your intention is the only thing that you have control over. After that, you need to respond to the customer in front of you and on what they are saying. If they're on the same page as you, and they're totally behind what you have suggested as the agenda, you move on to the next letters: A and L.

A & L = ASKING & LEARNING

Tina's training had been industry-specific, and this is where it had started to unravel for her. Rather than focusing on the customer, she had a set list of 'pains' to uncover — a bit like a problem treasure hunt of poking around and asking questions until the customer agreed that was a problem for them. Asking should be all about finding out about the customer, their situation, and how you might be able to help. There will be specific things you will need to know each time to figure out their circumstances, but your customers' needs have to come from your customer, in their own words.

Tina was regularly using what I call 'leading language' to get a customer to confirm that they are experiencing a problem. Not only can this result in you focusing on a problem that isn't actually a major problem for your customer, it will also very easily make your customer feel manipulated and not listened to. The main issue for Tina with this approach was that it wasn't her natural style; she wasn't someone who generally focused on the negative. She was so much better at talking about the positive and encouraging her clients — which is why her customers loved her so much — and that's what she needed to do in her calls.

The first question a potential customer is often asked is a friendly, open question. You are looking to get top-line background information on their situation. In most cases, this may take some time and you might need to delve a little deeper to obtain further information and get clarification.

The next set of questions tends to 'signpost' the person. For example, when I sell for the agency, there are two distinct types of sell:

1. Selling to those who have run paid advertising before
2. Selling to those who have not run paid advertising before

A lot of my clients need to understand a potential customer's breadth of knowledge on a subject in order to sell to them effectively. That might not be the case for your business, but more often than not, it is a deciding factor in the approach you need to take.

Back when I started working with small-business owners, I worked with a lady called Pam. She was a fantastic doula and sought after in her field. She would get many enquiries but was struggling to convert them into paying customers. On talking through her sales calls, it became clear she wasn't tailoring the information at all to the person she was talking to. At the end of the call, she hadn't uncovered why her potential customer wanted to use her or what had motivated them to seek out a doula. Therefore, most of her enquiries led to nothing, and potential customers ended the call without feeling heard or understood. They also weren't being told how she could meet their needs; they were just getting a list of features around a very personal and emotional decision.

We looked in more detail at what was going wrong for Pam in her sales call, and found that it started right at the beginning of her call with a very common mistake: she jumped straight into talking about what she does and how she can help, without finding out enough information about what was motivating her customers.

We put into place a series of 'signposting' questions to determine her customers' motivations. Because there were two distinct background scenarios of Pam's clients — first-time parents and parents with children already — we devised a simple question to determine if they had given birth before. From this question, the call went in two clear trajectories: first-timers were interested in having the best experiences, while the others wanted to avoid repeating a past bad experience.

Their needs were totally different. Once we understood what motivated them, based on their background, the call became about exploring their needs and identifying how Pam could help them.

I WORRY I WILL ANNOY PEOPLE WITH QUESTIONS

After doing sales calls repeatedly, you might feel you're asking the same question all the time. You are. That's because you're talking about the same subject matter, but you're not talking to or asking these questions to the same people. This is why Learning ('L') is so important in this process. You might be bored of asking the questions and listening to the answers, but for the potential customer you are talking to, this is the first time they have considered these questions. This element of the sales conversation, the asking and learning phase, should take up to 70 percent of the call, if not more, because this is your opportunity to really get to know this person.

That is not to say there is no danger of annoying your customer! The main reasons people get frustrated by questions are when the questions aren't linked, there is no obvious value to them, and the person asking them doesn't seem to be taking the answers on board. On the other hand, when you're drilling down with specific, relevant questions, the customer understands why you're doing it and can see the direction you're going. Sometimes, if people don't like that direction, or they see that you're barking up the wrong tree, they will tell you. That's okay — the point is, you're learning where that person's at.

Asking for clarification on people's answers stops them from feeling as though they are being cross-examined. Deeper questioning is also essential to fully understand where your ideal customer is coming from, what they actually mean, and what is driving their needs, preferences, and opinions. So, if you need to know more about that question, delve down into the subject and find out more from the customer. Don't leave potentially vital information hanging there; gain those insights. Once you have clarity on the subject, a great way to ensure you understand what they are saying is by repeating the key points back to the client using your own words and then checking you are right. If a customer says something you aren't sure about, don't ever leave yourself wondering and don't ever fill in the blanks. Ask them for clarity. Learn as much as you can.

Tina had a list of common pains her clients had, and she had been trained to work through the list from start to finish. Never ask questions for the sake of asking questions. You're asking questions to learn about that customer. Again, this tick-box exercise can easily cause a customer to feel unheard and manipulated. If your questions are steering a customer to a specific topic on your agenda, that topic is not necessarily theirs. The key thing is to find out what their key priorities are — not yours!

All those ideas you had about your ideal customer on paper may be challenged by the person sitting in front of you or on the end of the line. Not only are you determining whether they are your ideal customer and fit for your offering, you're also building a more complete ideal-customer avatar; you can never know too much about them. You can always add information. You can always add opinions. You can always take quotes from them to understand them better and where they're coming from. Always keep learning.

QUESTIONS FOR YOUR TOOLKIT

There are three types of questions to use in this phase of the call: situational, open, and closed.

Situational questions help you to understand better the circumstances that surround your customer — the information you need to build a clear picture of where they are coming from. The plus for you is that you can get some background information. The answers tend to be facts and figures, not thoughts or feelings.

The negative for customers is that this sort of question doesn't hold much value; they are not exploring anything, and you're not helping them to develop an understanding of anything. And so, you want to limit those situational questions. They are useful to you for market research and targeting, not your customer — remember this.

Examples:

- How long have you been in this role?
- How long has the business been running?
- How many staff do you have?
- What is your turnover?
- Who makes the decisions?

Open questions give your customer free rein to talk about what is important to them or whatever is at the forefront of their mind on that subject. These can enable you to get an understanding of their thought processes, rationale, and prior decisions they made that got them to that point. The drawback of an open question is that you can go off on tangents and you might get irrelevant information that detracts from the main focus of the call. You may need to bring the customer back on track, acknowledging what they have said whilst getting them to refocus. One open question that Tina decided to use for the start of her calls was, 'What motivated you to make a change now?' The responses are normally very subjective, i.e., based on feeling and emotion.

Examples:

- What do you enjoy most about your job?
- What's your biggest challenge in your business right now?
- What impact does that challenge have on you?
- What would be your perfect job?

Closed questions can be answered with a simple yes or no. It's difficult to get the same level of insight, or even get the conversation going with a closed question, so should only be used to confirm what the potential customer has said. If someone doesn't want to talk, asking them closed questions won't help them to open up.

Examples:

- Do you enjoy your job?
- Is losing weight important to you?
- Does being overweight make you feel self-conscious?

Sometimes closed questions can work well as a first-stage question, especially when looking to signpost a potential customer towards one conversation or another. If you back up their 'yes' or 'no' response with questions that delve deeper into the subject, then they can be quite useful. For Tina, the weight loss coach, she needed to know if that person had tried a weight loss plan before. The vast majority of her customers had, but she needed to know for sure, so her follow-up questions were around what sort of plans they had tried before. Without further encouragement, the person is unlikely to elaborate.

Where possible, change closed questions into open ones. 'Do you like cake?' is clearly a closed question. Asking them what their favourite type of baked treat is will give you a much better insight into how much they like cake in comparison to other options. From there you can go on to ask them where cake fits into their preferences, getting a much more accurate opinion of what they think of it.

In short:

- Open questions offer the potential to learn something new from your customer.
- Closed questions confirm something you have (or think you have) already learned from your customer.

TREAT EVERY TIME LIKE THE FIRST TIME

Your customers probably all have the same problem. They probably have the same background. They more than likely provide the same information and have experienced the same challenges.

But the customer you're talking to for the first time hasn't told you this before. It's really important that customers don't like feeling like you have heard it all before, and 'it's the same old story.' The key here is to fully understand them first before you reassure them that you deal with this sort of thing all the time: never cut short their outpouring of information.

When you are dealing with the same situation day in, day out, it is very easy to jump in and start problem-solving. However, if the customer doesn't feel like you have totally listened, they aren't going to be receptive to your solution. Instead, sit tight and give them that time to talk through their scenario, show them respect, and find out what is going on for them. You don't want to miss out on an opportunity because you've decided that it's a little bit boring to listen to somebody talk through the same problems you hear from all your other customers. Sometimes your role as a salesperson can get very close to being a counsellor — particularly when you're talking about challenges they are facing. But if you have run out of empathy for your ideal customer, perhaps it's time to rethink your career!

BRINGING THINGS BACK ON TRACK

As mentioned previously, when asking open questions, there is the potential that your customer will go off topic — especially if you start talking about challenges in their business or role. Believe it or not, your customer has a lot more to think about than just the subjects that relate to your product! Fortunately, these moments are a great insight into your customers' world and, significantly, their priorities.

When I was selling wound-care products (fancy dressing for wounds bigger than you want to imagine) I was part of a highly trained sales team. They gave us the most training I have ever experienced during my lifetime as a salesperson. We fully understood the biggest challenges of our customer base weeks before we were let loose to speak to them. We would practice relating their biggest challenges, such as staffing, which seemed totally irrelevant to wound-care dressings, to the products' performance. So how did we relate staffing shortage to dressings? The benefit we were able to relate was our product's 'wear time': the dressings were super absorbent and could be kept on for up to seven days. An extended wear time meant that they weren't required to be changed so often, therefore helping with the staffing issues.

It's a tenuous link, perhaps, but it worked because it was a genuine benefit of the product, and it was a logical solution to their problem. It is always worth thinking about your product or service's impact on the bigger picture, be it budget, human resources, or equipment. Sometimes conversations go totally off-piste, covering topics that in no way relate to your product. Or it covers enough to show that their problem can't be solved by any of your features or benefits — in which case, you need to refocus the conversation.

The risk of derailing a call with an open question is something Tina and a lot of my clients have struggled with and worry most about when talking to customers. We have all been there when a customer has gone off on a tangent and you can't get them back on track. So, here are a few tips to help you.

- **Acknowledge the situation your customer is faced with.** Show empathy, if you are someone who naturally shows empathy. If not, try offering a positive perspective on their problem. To some people, this can be annoying, but you're not trying to please everyone. Trying to be empathetic when you really aren't capable of it comes across as totally insincere!

- **Acknowledge the limits of your expertise.** Explain that their challenge isn't your area of expertise, but that you can help them in other ways.

- **Be helpful by making referrals.** If you have any resources (contacts or other customers who have overcome that challenge), or professional associates who could help, then suggest them and ask if you can make the connection.

- **Get back on topic — lead the conversation.** Acknowledge what they have said, get clarity on what they have said, if needed, and then bring them back to the focus of the conversation, using the SALES acronym to help you determine where in the call structure you need to restart. Note: This may have to be done repeatedly; if so, you can also make the customer aware of the time constraints and/or how you are mindful of covering everything.

Having her own version of these responses really helped Tina to relax and feel more in control. Six months on from our time together, she has only had to use them once, but it's knowing what to do in these situations that enables you to feel more confident on calls. With confidence comes respect and control of the conversation so it never goes too far off on a tangent.

*Having obtained all the information we need to determine how
we can best help her ideal customer, Tina and I moved on to
work on E and S of SALES (Explaining and Steps), which we are going to
cover in the next chapter. Before then, fill out the
PDF worksheet whilst this is all fresh in your mind so you, too,
can confidently ask questions and learn from your customer
whilst feeling in control: available at
www.sellingwithoutsleaze.com/bookresources.*

SECTION IV:

CLOSE

9

WHY YOU, WHY NOW?

(THE PART CALLED 'PITCHING')

Using the process and hints and tips in Chapter 8, you have identified key priorities for your customer, you have understood what their needs (or wants) are, and you know that your product can help them. Based on the information obtained during the Asking and Learning phases, you should know at least one (ideally two or three) top needs your customer has that you can address. If this isn't the case and you're struggling to find needs that relate to your product — or needs you are able to meet — then take another look at Chapter 8 because it forms the foundation of this section and makes your life much easier.

With your ideal customer's top needs prioritised in your mind, we can move on to the next letter of SALES, which is Explaining. Explaining is your opportunity to tell your customer how you and/or your product can help. To illustrate, I'll continue Tina's story from Chapter 8, keeping things nice and simple to follow.

E = EXPLAINING (THE 'SELLING' BIT)

From the needs you've uncovered, you obviously choose the most relevant issues to work on. Ideally, these will align with your USPs and will set your product or service apart from the competition (more about selling against your competition later in the chapter). In doing so, you are providing the potential customer with the most compelling reasons for working with you — based on their priorities and your strengths.

As we saw with Tina, it is essential that the customer volunteers the information about their most important needs. If they were led to providing the information and confirm the need, your life gets very difficult during the explaining stage. Working through and explaining how you can help with a need that the customer genuinely has will mean your potential customer will be so much more engaged. If you can truly meet their needs, you are explaining a solution to their 'problem', and who wouldn't be interested in that?

When you are selling for your business all the time, this is easy. You are talking about the same problems and solutions day in, day out because your product meets a particular set of needs or wants. That means you can be fully prepared for this part. You might need to adapt elements of your explanation to each client, but you will be able to use the same phrases, descriptions, and metaphors to convey how you and your product can help the client.

The reason I mention metaphors here is because they are really useful. When I worked in medical sales, I used a whole range of metaphors for the different products and technologies because it brought it to life in a way that people could understand. For example, when I explain how most people who I work with get tired of searching around for customers that aren't even decent customers, I liken it to people panning for gold. During the Gold Rush, everyone was doing the same thing, scraping around at the bottom of the river trying to find tiny nuggets of gold. It was backbreaking, hard work, and they got few rewards for all their hard labour. While scraping around, they were not in control of the resources available to them. With more skills and knowledge, plus the right equipment, they could mine for the gold, which would have given them a much higher yield for their efforts. Efficiency AND control.

That metaphor brings home to my clients the fact that if they work smarter — if they target the right people and equip themselves with the right knowledge and tools to target those people — they wouldn't need to scrape around in the same way, trying to be heard over the noise of their competition. By investing in the right resources, you invest in the right approach, yielding better results.

The explaining element, like all the five key elements of SALES, is essential if a call is to be successful. You can learn all you want about a customer, you can ask as many questions as you like, but you need to put this information to good use. This is your specialist area and your opportunity to inform your customer about your product — why and how you can help them in relation to their needs. You always need to keep the focus on what your customers' needs are, not what you want them to be, which is where Tina was before we started working together.

Again, Tina would regularly push people towards the topics on her list of potential 'pains'. Listening in to the calls, it was clear how much the customer was being led. Most people are averse to confrontation and regularly agree just because it is the easiest thing to do. This can be highly detrimental in the Asking and Learning phase, as you can end up in a situation where you are explaining how you can help someone with a need that really isn't a priority to them. That's where Tina regularly found herself on her calls.

EXPLAINING IN YOUR OWN STYLE

The Selling Without Sleaze method is very much about selling your own style. The use of language throughout the call should be unique to you; I would always urge you to keep the style you want to communicate in as close to your natural style as possible. I appreciate you might want to 'clean up' your language a little if you are selling in a more professional environment — as if you are on your best behaviour at a relative's house — but you want to be you as much as possible.

The key challenge Tina had was with being herself. She became so robotic with the approach she had been taught, it took a lot of practice and me repeatedly asking, 'Would you say that to a friend?' and 'What would your partner think if they heard you saying that?' to get her thinking about how she would naturally talk. It took time, but we got there!

My advice to stay true to yourself isn't just because I'm on a one-woman crusade to help people be more authentic. I advise it because you will attract the people you want to work with, who you will enjoy working with more (because they will value your unique qualities), and you will get better results because you have a stronger relationship with them. And you will help those people make the decision to work with you sooner because they will be able to build trust with you quicker.

When I explain this to customers, I ask, 'What are your thoughts on that?' Other people, however, are more focused on feelings than on thoughts. If you favour a feelings approach, then you might be more likely to ask them how they feel about a particular topic. For me, that's very alien. I remember when I first started out in medical sales, I had a manager who always encouraged me to ask people, 'How does that make you feel?' This was so uncomfortable because it just wasn't a question I would naturally ask. In fact, I felt quite dirty asking it; it was just too personal, too intrusive a question to ask people I didn't know well. I much preferred to ask them what they thought. Whatever your preference, the outcome to the question about thoughts or feelings is the same: you will get a reading on that person that indicates where they are at and if they are on board with what you are saying.

Once you've got that insight and they are on board, you are able to progress to discussing next steps. If that person needs a little more convincing before they will be happy to move on, you will be able to use this phase to get clarity on what they need to feel confident about progressing to the next stage.

For example, when I talk to clients, I describe how another client achieved a 506 percent increase in sales by working with me and then maintained that level of sales. After detailing this and relating it to the potential client's need to increase sales, I ask them what their thoughts are. One response I get is, 'Well that's all well and good for that person, but my service is totally different.' My response at this point isn't, 'Great, let's get you signed up' because that just wouldn't make any sense. I need to understand what *would* make them feel more confident. My response, therefore, goes something like, 'Would it help if I went through a case study with a similar offering to yourself?' I then go through it and check again what their thoughts are. It is important at this stage to be aware of where the client is in the process and to keep things progressing at a suitable pace for them.

If you try and railroad someone by sticking to your own agenda regardless of what they're saying or failing to listen, that's when they feel like you don't understand them. This is the basis of their suspicion that you're just trying to push them into something that doesn't work for them. Not everybody will have a single conversation before deciding to sign on the dotted line — particularly when you're talking about high ticket price items.

ADAPT YOUR EXPLANATION FOR THE CUSTOMER

Ideal or not, the customer in front of you is the person you are talking to, so use their language and talk at their level. I don't mean patronise them! I mean, use the information they have provided to you in the A and L section of the call to determine what information is important to them and what can be missed out.

Tina loved to talk about the exact process her clients would go through. That's great if that's important to the customer, but not if they didn't care about the process, only the result. If they only care about results, then that's what you talk about. Think about the last time you bought something technical (such as a computer or TV). Unless the salesperson was decent, you probably got a list of technical features (such as the amount of RAM or pixels), and maybe you got a bit of an explanation as to what the feature means. It is unlikely they uncovered any of your needs prior to launching into the details. This positions the salesperson as a walking brochure, and you end up with even more information than you started with but no further clarity on what that means to you.

Talk through how you can help your potential customer with their specific needs. If they want to mount a screen/monitor on the wall, then talk to them about the easiest one to mount, or the best size for the room and position they want to put it in. If they want to edit music on their computer, describe what they need a computer to do to give them the ability to do that easily and which product provides that.

Once Tina uncovered the customers' actual needs, and which were her priority, then there was no stopping her. She knew how effective she was at getting results for clients and had a catalogue of case studies to talk through, so she simply needed to choose the right case study for the potential client's need and explain the impact she could have on them. You will often find with sales that once one thing clicks into place, things come much easier — just like it did for Tina.

S = STEPS TO BE AGREED

There will potentially be multiple conversations — probably with different decision makers — so understand what steps are in the decision-making process and make recommendations based on your knowledge to guide them through it. If you are unsure of the next step because you don't know what is involved from their point of view, ask! Gain from them an understanding of what their situation and processes are and go from there.

Tina's clients tended to have to run things past their other halves to make sure they were happy with them spending a sizable amount on weight management. We worked through the best way to support her customer in doing this. She basically needed to equip them to sell on her behalf to their partners. Historically, Tina had been trained to push them to make a decision on the call using a special offer only available if they signed up there and then, and then to challenge them about why they would need to get permission from their other half — eek!

Not only was this approach counterproductive, some people just weren't in a position to make a decision there and then — no matter the pressure or offer used. It was rude, and it didn't do Tina justice at all. She was a lovely, empathetic person. On the call recordings, I could tell she was clearly awkward and embarrassed to put the pressure on. Never, ever say or do anything in your business you don't feel comfortable with. It is your business and your customer base — it's down to you to protect them.

Figure out how to help the client through their unique situations. The key thing is you are giving them a task and a reason to keep the conversation going. The next step might be to send them some information to read in their own time and set up a call to discuss what they've read.

You are getting a task (setting up the call) and they are getting a task (doing some reading). It's not all the responsibility of the customer, and, equally, not all your responsibility. Effort on both sides demonstrates sufficient buy-in from both parties to make the relationship work. If they're not investing time or money in moving it forward, how invested are they really? So, get them to do something and show commitment.

Always agree to timescales and stick to them. This is potentially the first time they will experience what it is like to work with you, and so you want them to be able to come away from that experience with a positive outlook. Ensure you are giving them a positive experience, and be sure to stick to your deadlines and do what you say you're going to do.

SELLING AGAINST THE COMPETITION

At this stage in the sales call, it may be an option to sell against a competitor. However, I should say that I am not a fan of selling yourself on someone else's shortcomings (i.e., 'competitor X doesn't do this'). It is by far better to point out your merits and simply equip your ideal customer to ask the right questions of your competitors if they are shopping around. Prioritise the areas that are your USPs so that your ideal customer sees them as their key priorities too.

When I sell for the agency, I am clear with potential customers about the price they will pay for different levels of paid traffic support. Straight away this provides them with knowledge and the ability to question other people's services. It also makes them look at products and services more closely if someone else appears more competitive on price, but I have already forewarned them of the logical reasons our support isn't cheap.

Our agency also has an in-house team of creatives. This is not something most of our competitors have, so there is more onus on clients to create (or pay for) images and videos to be created. I talk through the value of this with potential customers and the impact it has on their budget and ad performance. Again, it is educating them about how our service works and the value for money they receive. It also prioritises in their heads the need for an in-house creative team, so that becomes something they look for in a potential supplier.

I am, in effect, enabling potential customers to ask the right questions that will highlight our USPs, and help them realise why we are the best solution. This might sound manipulative, but if you honestly and truly believe in what you are selling, then you know that you would be doing your potential customer a disservice not to let them know the key things to look for.

All too often we receive enquiries from people who have been ripped off or taken advantage of by companies that charge a monthly fee to run the most basic of ads (as few as two per month), which they let run for months at a time without making any changes whatsoever. These companies give the industry a bad name and leave potential customers feeling understandably cheated and suspicious of other suppliers. It's not right, so I feel a moral obligation to give people some idea of what to look out for and urge them to train themselves to a basic level on the subject of paid traffic, so they have a foundational understanding of what they don't know. I advise you to do the same.

*It's time to look at what your ideal customers' needs are likely to be and the go-to phrases you are going to use to explain how you can meet those needs. So, go to the website to download your worksheet to get these 'tools' in your toolkit at **www.sellingwithoutsleaze.com/bookresources**.*

10

FOLLOWING UP

(DON'T FALL AT THE FINAL FENCE)

In medical sales, there is an expectation that you follow up with potential clients, but I have to admit that follow-ups and cold calling were my least favourite elements of sales. However, having stuck at it, out of necessity, I can now genuinely say I love following up (although I am still learning to love the cold calling).

For me, following up is now just part of the process and so it comes more naturally. For the version of me who started in sales, however, there was nothing natural about it. It felt forced and awkward, like I was checking up on the customer to make sure that they had done what they said. The main reason I have come to love the follow-up is because I have seen the impact it continues having over the years and, more recently, on mine and my clients' businesses.

I cannot emphasise enough the importance of following up. The vast majority of your potential clients now have stakeholders they need to talk to when making decisions, or they want to shop around, or they want to gain more information — particularly when you're talking about higher priced items. Understandably, people have become more suspicious and cautious when it comes to buying decisions. Bad experiences and horror stories of people getting ripped off are rife — especially in the online world where I tend to hang out and attract clients. It's only right that people want to do their homework before committing — it makes total sense!

Even with low-price items, people want clarity on what they are getting. Audiences, particularly in the online business operations space, are getting increasingly cautious. They've had a lot of people promise the earth but haven't delivered, having sold them something that actually doesn't work for their needs. I see it a lot. This often means people need to go away and think about your offer; they need to find out further information and consult people.

Thinking about your ideal customer, you want to be reflecting on who they use to make a decision — who they consult, what resources they use — and ensure you've got 'touch points' on there. For example, if your customer uses Trustpilot (or any online review app), make sure you're on there. Not only that, make sure that you're featured and ensure there's information there which is accurate about you. Dr Jeffrey Lant, the marketing psychology expert, talks about the 'Rule of Seven' (1992, *Cash Copy*, Jeffrey Lant Associates): it takes at least seven touch points before you enter the buyer's consciousness. To be honest, I'm surprised it's not more than that.

It's therefore safe to say that you cannot expect a purchase to occur during that initial conversation. It is highly unlikely that they decide to buy from you the first time they talk to you. It takes multiple touch points. People are being exposed to more and more brands in a busy market, so it therefore takes more touch points to get their attention and build the trust in you that your ideal customer must have in order to buy from you.

There's a lot of potential business still left on the table at the end of a call. A sale is not lost if it isn't closed during the first call; it's lost by a lack of timely follow-up. At least 80 percent of the people I work with hadn't been following up consistently before I started working with them. They know they *should* follow up, but they don't do it.

WHAT IS FOLLOW-UP?

The term applies to scenarios after you've started a conversation about working together, or how your business might be able to help your potential customer, and they have expressed interest. At this point, you're in a position to provide them with information they can read up on or use to carry out further research.

Do whatever it takes for them to feel more confident about making a decision. It might be that you need to provide more information. It might be that they want to research stuff or talk to somebody. Whatever it is that you've decided as the next step at the end of the call, the important thing is to take action.

When I was starting out in medical sales, I would give potential clients a sample of one of the dressings I sold, to try on a patient whom we had identified as suitable during the call. The follow-up for me was to get them to actually put it on the patient and then provide feedback as to how it went. This sounds straightforward enough, but it actually involved a lot of chasing them down for feedback. Customers were not getting back to me, nor were they implementing their side of the process, either due to changes in circumstance or simply forgetting. Nevertheless, I persisted!

Not everyone takes action at this point. The normal response of most of my clients (before working with me) was to allow a potential customer to go off and try the product, or talk to a family member, friend, or colleague, without any clear indication of a timescale. Therefore, the onus of responsibility for getting back into contact was on the potential customer and, unsurprisingly, my clients never heard from those potential customers again.

Straight away, I set new parameters with clients as to what is and isn't acceptable when it comes to next steps. At the end of the call, you need to know what timescale the potential customer is working to for a decision to be made, and why they are working to that timescale. If there are other decision makers in the process, try and organise a call with them. If that isn't possible, then it's essential to fully understand the influence of the other decision makers, and what information they want to see, and then equip the potential customer with the information they need to convince them. Finally, you need to understand when your contact person will speak to the gatekeeper, and from there organise a time within the following 24 hours to speak to them again.

People often worry this is too pushy. When taking account of your customers' timescales, all you are doing is matching your level of assertiveness to the timescales they have stated. You are taking them at their word and supporting them to meet their deadline. What is wrong with that?

To maximise the number of sales, you need to maintain the momentum of the sale. The world is a busy place! If the sales process is too drawn out, something else becomes a priority and the sale loses energy. The potential customer no longer feels that same pain, so no longer feels that same motivation to rectify their problem and address it with your solution. So, the key here is to keep those follow-up timescales as short as possible. If somebody's speaking to a confidant that afternoon, there's no reason you shouldn't be able to speak to them that evening, or the following morning. It is as short as that. And what you're trying to do is keep the conversation going. There is no need to leave it days and days so that they don't remember the ins and outs of the conversation with you. Keep those times nice and tight.

This is, again, an opportunity for your customer to understand what it would be like to work with you. Who doesn't want to work with somebody who's motivated and driven to move a project along? This won't reflect badly on you. If they do feel like you're being pushy, they'll push back and let you know that, actually: 'I don't want to speak to you today. I want to speak to you next week.' There's nothing wrong at that point with asking why they want that extra space. Most of the time, it's because they want to think something through or get some other quotes. When asked nicely, most people are open to telling you that. Of course, if they aren't, don't push it. But take note: it is likely a sign that they have reservations or aren't as bought-in as you had hoped.

Hopefully the message here is super obvious. Always follow up! And where possible, always agree to a day and time for that follow-up so you can put it in the diary. Send a calendar invite to them to make it 'official', reducing the risk of a no-show and keeping the momentum of the sale going.

ACCOUNT MANAGEMENT: NOW YOU'VE GOT THEM, KEEP THEM

Account management is basically maintaining a business relationship with a customer who has bought from you. It is important to do this for three reasons.

1. Keeping up to date

First, you want to keep in regular contact with them so that it's easy for them to work with you again, particularly when you're introducing new products or services. Maintaining contact makes sense, so that you can pick up where you left off quickly.

There's also scope to point them in the direction of other professionals and resources that can help them. Affiliates are often professionals with whom you have a mutually beneficial referral relationship, but they can also be in the form of services. For example, I have an affiliate link to my Customer Relationship Manager (CRM) system. I love our CRM system, so I have no problem promoting it to my clients for use in their businesses. I would recommend my CRM provider regardless of whether I got an affiliate kickback (a monetary return), but as I do get a kickback, it's a nice reward for giving them recognition. Think about who you would be happy referring clients to, and if the person or company doesn't have a clear referral process, get in touch and ask. Equally, if you can think of people who could refer their clients to you, or do already refer people to you, then get something more official in place that everyone can benefit from.

2. Understanding more customers

Secondly, account management helps you understand that customer. And the more you understand that customer, the more you can understand other customers. The more useful you can be to them, the more rapport you can build with your audience. It's basically zero-cost market research involving someone who has already bought from you. These relationships make a massive difference.

3. Seeking further opportunities

Lastly, effective account management helps you seek out other opportunities. It is not just about cross-selling; you're up-selling, or you're affiliate-selling.

Going back to my time in the pharmaceutical industry, I remember sitting with a customer and talking about a highly specialist drug that my company produced. They told me, 'It's really useful to have it in this format and available to us on this ward, but actually that isn't the drug we use the most.' I asked some questions and got an understanding of the potential volume and dosage of the other drug they would need, and I asked about other drugs that would be useful in that format, which was quicker, safer, and easier to use. I was able to feed that data back to the research and development team and, as a business, we were able to provide what was needed in the desired format. We wouldn't have known anything about the potential of that drug presentation had it not been for that conversation. The drug was a generic, and we went from being one of many who provided it to the only one providing it in that special format. So, you can imagine the increase in usage that we got. It was a very profitable product development!

From the customer's point of view, we had gone away to design a product that met their specific need and solve a problem. Guess who they're going to talk to the next time they have a challenge or a problem? This shows that building that strong customer relationship — working closely together on a professional basis — can be invaluable and very profitable for your business.

You have spent time and money obtaining a customer, so it makes sense to maximise the return on that investment and capitalise on the relationship that you have created. Aside from any additional revenue you may be able to generate, what's the point in creating a fantastic and sustainable relationship only to neglect it?

Within the medical devices market, my customer became my currency. They were the value I brought to a new company when they employed me. There's a saying that 'your network is your net worth', and in sales that is totally true. Companies paid more for me because I had established relationships with clients they needed to build relationships with. This is a fantastic position to be in. However, while you do end up being valued very highly in your niche, moving niches requires you to be realistic (your value is going to be downgraded and so will your pay). The value of contacts is as significant for small businesses as it is for larger organisations, which is another reason to look after those ideal customers.

To help you plan your follow-up approach,
download the PDF worksheet at
www.sellingwithoutsleaze.com/bookresources.

CONCLUSION:

CREATING YOUR SALES TOOLKIT

Yay! You made it to the end of the book! Unless of course you flicked straight to the end, in which case, don't be lazy — get back to the beginning!

Over the past ten chapters, I have shared hints, tips, and real-life examples of actions you can be taking in your business right now to generate more sales without acting out of character or resorting to sleazy techniques. Now it's time to take action and get yourself off that hamster wheel of implementation.

Each chapter has an activity at the end of it designed to help you begin creating your toolkit. This is something I work on with all my clients so that they have go-to resources to use for their unique ideal customer and/or personal communication style. I'm not claiming that you will be able to create all the resources you could possibly need simply by using the worksheets and lessons from each chapter. However, there is enough in this book to get you started and, most significantly, to make changes in your business right now. Putting the information together and making the most of the information you glean from the worksheets will help you create the foundations of your sales toolkit. This includes your tried and tested responses, questions, and resources that you use to support your ideal customer through the sales process and show how you can meet their needs.

The basic principles of TACC are at the centre of this book and form the basis of this toolkit. Remember, the TACC system is designed to help you easily remember the elements you need so you can get in front of and convert your ideal customers, helping you create a business you enjoy.

We started out in Chapter 1 with T for Target, providing a focus for your goals — most significantly your financial goals. Understanding, prioritising, and working towards a clearly defined goal enables you to measure your performance and have a clear direction. This should help you to keep on track. A helpful addition to this can be to have an account-ability buddy; this relationship can help you both stay focused.

We then moved on to explore your ideal customer. The questions I got you answering on the worksheet are the tip of the iceberg. I walk clients through many more questions in one-to-one sessions, but answering the basic questions in this chapter will give you a great foundation for understanding your ideal customer better. Time and time again, the struggles of the people I speak to come back to not knowing their ideal customer well enough to be able to predict their ideal customer's needs. Focusing and revisiting the questions on the worksheet will really help you to stay in tune with your ideal customer — understanding who they are and what their current needs are.

Chapter 3 puts a magnifying glass to your market and competition, looking at how you compare, what makes you unique, and why your customers should buy from you and not your competition. I totally appreciate these are the tricky questions, but they are much better addressed in the worksheet than they are when you are in front of a potential customer!

Chapters 4 to 6 focused on the approach. You couldn't start approaching people without first addressing that buzzword: mindset. Mindset can affect your approach to sales, and it can even stop you from achieving more. The worksheet for this chapter is designed to give you that mental boost when it comes to remembering how great you are, the value you bring to customers, and that you know your stuff! It also paves the way for you to explore opportunities within your market right now, exercising the creative side of your brain and seeing the positives.

You can have great ideas, appear super useful and knowledgeable, but if you don't make it as easy as possible for people to understand how they can work with you, they can end up going elsewhere — that's what Chapter 5 was all about. Knowing where your solutions fit, both within the market and in comparison to your competition, is vital if you are going to successfully meet and resolve your ideal customer's needs and secure your business and its position in the market for the long term. Answering the questions at the end of this chapter can be a harsh wake-up call — or a pleasant confirmation of how great you are and how on-point your offering is. Either way, it's best to know where you stand so you know the work that needs to be done to make it as easy as possible for your ideal customer to work with you.

Chapter 6 went through the steps that can make the communication stage of TACC easier: tailoring your approach to your customer.

Considering, in detail, the stages that your ideal customer needs to go through before they will feel comfortable buying, as well as considering what you might want to put in place to facilitate or speed up that process, could make a massive impact not only on your sales volume but also how much it costs you to acquire that customer.

With all the preparation done, it's then time to communicate with your ideal customer on a more one-to-one basis. This is the juicy sales bit, where we talked through the sales 'call'. Chapter 7 gave you an introduction to the SALES process (**Stating** the reason for the call, **Asking** questions and **Learning** about your ideal customer before **Explaining** how you can help and agreeing what the next **Steps** are to progress the buying relationship), which I created to sell without sleaze.

Just like dating, it's all about getting to know your ideal customer and understanding what they need. Having clarity on how you are going to structure a call will enable you to be more effective. It's easy for customer conversations to run away with you, so in Chapter 8, I went through how to take control and find out the information you need to provide value to your ideal customer. Understanding their needs and motivations means you can make recommendations on the suitability of your product/service for them whilst being mindful of how you make them feel. There's also scope here to go that one step further and create your go-to phrases and questions to use in the call to be even more effective.

We are then onto the final stage of TACC: the close.

You need to make it clear why the potential customer should use you to meet their needs and why they should do it now. Providing that sense of urgency helps your ideal customer move forwards in the sales process, but it is an area where lots of people become unstuck. Using what you learned in Chapter 9 will enable you to sell effectively without being sleazy, helping your customers move along that sales process. Again, deploying go-to phrases and examples at this stage will grow your sales toolkit and help you be more effective.

Speaking of effectiveness, I cannot stress how important the follow-up is, especially in today's busy world. That's why I dedicated the whole of Chapter 10 to it! I hope you learned in this section that it's not all about the sales call. Lots of sales are made during the follow-up. The value in following up isn't just in sales; it's also in the form of feedback. Focusing on the follow-up and getting as much feedback and information as possible from potential customers you have spoken to can be truly invaluable. Although I can appreciate it can also be a painful process, I promise you do get used to it! Detaching yourself personally from the feedback means you can make the most of it, and if you act on it, you can also avoid the same feedback again.

IMPROVE AND EVOLVE

Sales is a skill that is never completely 'ticked off' as done. Your ideal customer is always evolving — products and markets evolve — so it's super important you treat this as an ongoing process from regularly checking in on your ideal customer's priorities to consistently reviewing your call techniques.

I used to accompany members of the sales team, with over 35 years of experience in sales, on visits to customers. Some of these were professional salespeople who had spent their entire careers selling within the same market, nearing retirement. You might think they were happy to 'coast' through the last few years. In fact, they were some of the most motivated and conscientious salespeople I had ever met. On reflection, that shouldn't have been surprising, as they had such a successful career in sales because of their willingness to continuously improve and evolve. They still outperformed the younger members of the team due to the knowledge and skills they had developed and their willingness to receive feedback and to improve. I remember one of them saying, 'Even if these changes get me a *yes* five minutes quicker, that's ten minutes between me and the customer we are saving on every call.' And that's the key thing about sales: it's the tweaks and changes that add up.

My aims with my programme, Selling Without Sleaze, are to change people's perceptions of sales and feel less alienated and turned off by the prospect of selling. It would be fantastic if people felt more at home selling. If you develop a toolkit of skills and resources that you can use for your ideal customer that is unique to you, then what you do and say will become more familiar and more natural. With this growing experience, you will feel more confident and become more effective at selling. I know this because I have seen it work time and time again in so many different industries.

WORKING WITH ME

I know there is enough in this book to get you started on making significant changes in your sales approach and, in time, your business growth. For some of you keen to move on to other areas of your business that need attention, this change will be enough for now.

For those of you who are hungry to learn more, hone your sales skills, and develop a full toolkit of resources to call upon when targeting, approaching, communicating, and closing your dream sale, there is additional support available. And as my clients will tell you, the training I provide soon pays for itself. Although the skills are for life, you don't have to wait a lifetime to see a return; most clients (more than 65 percent) make the investment back in increased sales whilst still on the course.

I love working with people who are good at what they do, but what 'they do' isn't sales and marketing. I love working with them to break through the revenue glass ceiling hanging over their business. Saying that, I also enjoy getting stuck in with less established or concept-stage businesses. The thing they all have in common? A willingness to embrace the process and put in the work required.

Tweaks and changes can often see those established businesses smash through that ceiling in no time, which gives me a massive buzz. However, if I had the chance to work with these people earlier, not only would I have saved them thousands of pounds but — as my track record has proven — I could have helped them to get that difficult-to-secure first client within six weeks, saving them time and money. That's why I find it so rewarding to help a new business navigate around the financial black holes, which normally take the form of shiny new website and business branding, and advertising.

Will you have enough time to make the most of the training? Feedback from clients is that the training isn't time consuming; in fact, most of the time it just replaces or complements the work you are already committed to doing (or should be committing to) in your business.

However, commitment to the process and consistent implementation is key, but don't worry: we help keep you focused and motivated. That's where my training programmes differ from others: the accountability is firm but fair and second to none. There's no point learning things if you don't then implement them.

I run a range of programmes, from one-to-one coaching to hybrid digital and group programmes. All programmes have an element of individual contact, however, because that's how we get results. We spend time on *you* and *your business*, helping you create *your sales toolkit* to sell *your offering* to *your ideal customer*. All the programmes are full on and, therefore, not for the faint-hearted. However, if you are serious about getting results, we will support you all the way to ensure you achieve your goals. The success of my clients is proof that if you put in the hard work of implementing what you learn then you will get results using the TACC approach.

If this sounds like you, then head over to www.sellingwithoutsleaze. com to find out more. Due to the one-to-one and intensively supportive nature of the programmes I offer, there are a limited number of spaces to work with me available at any one time; we therefore run a waiting list. If you or your business isn't ready, for whatever reason, to embark on one of my training programmes, we will not take your money. That is the Selling Without Sleaze ethos!

WHAT NEXT?

Please do say hi! Give me your feedback on the book or share with me your goals. I genuinely love hearing from people who have taken the time to develop their sales skills and invest in their personal and business growth — without the sleaze. Here's how you can find me.

- The best thing to do is head over to my website: www.sellingwithoutsleaze.com

- Check out the free content and reviews on my Facebook page: facebook.com/SarahJolleyJarvis.

- Watch some of my videos on YouTube: youtube.com/c/sarahjolleyjarvissellingwithoutsleaze.

- For those of you who like to get involved in 'proper conversations,' there's my free group 'Selling Without Sleaze' available here: facebook.com/groups/sellingwithoutsleaze.

- And for those that enjoy your content on the go, my podcast Selling Without Sleaze is available on the Apple and Spotify platforms.

HAPPY SELLING!

Printed in Great Britain
by Amazon

74933693R10078